THE REFERENCE SHELF (*Continued*)

THE REFERENCE SHELF

Vol. 24   No. 5

THE UNITED STATES
AND
INTERNATIONAL ORGANIZATIONS

Edited by

ROBERT E. SUMMERS

Assistant Professor of Journalism
University of Oregon

THE H. W. WILSON COMPANY
NEW YORK   1952

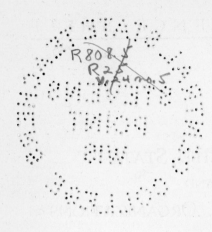

PREFACE

The political platforms adopted by the Democratic and Republican national conventions this year were remarkably alike with respect to foreign policy. Both parties pledged support of the United Nations and collective security arrangements. Major differences between the two parties appear to be in the methods used to implement foreign policy rather than disagreement in the basic philosophy. Since so much has happened in only the last two years in the realm of American foreign policy, the need to clarify some of the more important developments in this area has become more and more evident. In spite of political party unanimity on the subject of the United Nations and collective security, there is still considerable misunderstanding and disagreement as to this country's future role in participation in international organization.

It has been the purpose of the compiler to provide full background information on this country's present political commitments abroad and on the extent of American participation in various international organizations including the UN, and to outline briefly the nature of these various organizations and their purposes, in the hope of providing a better basis of understanding of the role this country may take in the future.

High school debaters are asked to discuss the general topic "What kind of international organization should the United States support?" The National University Extension Association statement of the question subdivides it into three discussion areas, each of which constitutes a possible substitute for the present course of action. The pros and cons of each proposal undoubtedly will be covered in detail in various other publications. This volume, however, is intended primarily as a first book in the study of the question, outlining American policies and some of the obstacles to the success of those policies. Space does not permit more than brief mention of the alternatives before the American people. Accordingly, this discussion is limited to those proposals which appear to have had the widest discussion in recent months. But there are a number of other proposals, among them Governor Thomas E. Dewey's program of regional defense for the whole of Southeast Asia as outlined in his recent volume *Journey to the Far Pacific*, and Senator Robert A. Taft's concept of "limited participation' which he expressed in his *Foreign Policy for Americans*. Since neither program has found majority support by the Republican party, in which both men hold positions of leadership, their views have been omitted in favor of those of Dwight D. Eisenhower, the Republican nominee, and Herbert Hoover, whose "Gibraltar of the West" proposal formed the basis of the Great Debate on foreign policy a little over a year ago.

It is hoped that the contents of this volume will throw light on the problems of American participation and make clear the nature of both the international and regional approaches to foreign policy which this country and its allies are pursuing at the present time.

The compiler is deeply indebted to Jack B. Cullen, director of the Ohio Speech League, and J. Steven Mills, graduate student in the Department of Speech, Ohio State University, for editorial assistance and criticism.

For their kindness in permitting reproduction of copyright materials appearing in the following pages, the compiler is deeply indebted to Messrs. Hanson W. Baldwin, Felix Belair, Jr., William G. Carleton, Thomas J. Hamilton, Michael L. Hoffman, James Reston, Beardsley Ruml, and C. L. Sulzberger; to the editors of the *AAUW Journal, Business Week, Christian Century, Collier's, Current History, Editorial Research Reports, Foreign Policy Reports, Foreign Affairs, Fortune,* the New York *Herald-Tribune,* the New York *Times, Political Science Quarterly, Reader's Digest, Virginia Quarterly Review, Vital Speeches,* and *World Affairs Interpreter;* and to the American Assembly, Graduate School of Business, Columbia University.

R. E. SUMMERS

August 1, 1952

CONTENTS

CONTENTS

CONTENTS

AMERICAN FOREIGN POLICY AT THE CROSSROADS

EDITOR'S INTRODUCTION

The United States today is in an extremely awkward position. Never before in history has a single nation attempted to do so much, assuming the multiple role of protector, adviser, banker and father confessor for a large part of the world. As self-avowed leader of the free world, the United States has assumed international commitments on a gigantic scale, attempting to build a world order on a firm basis of unity and cooperation. But the initiative has been chiefly American, the necessary financing has also been American, and the ultimate success of this "strong, free world" Americans visualize will depend largely upon policies that the United States pursues in the future.

This entails tremendous responsibilities. And to Americans new to the role of world leadership the situation is fraught with serious consequences, not only to this country, but to all nations who have accepted our leadership. After the end of fighting in World War II, the average American readily accepted the necessity of rebuilding war-torn Europe, of sending goods and money abroad to put Europe "on her feet." That was in the old American tradition and we had done it before. But it was more difficult to grasp the implications of political leadership.

Many Americans had assumed, optimistically, in 1945 that world "relief" and economic aid would be enough. National economies would soon be restored and everything would return to normal once more. Politically, the defeat of the Axis powers made it possible to think in terms of international organization—and the United Nations was created to end for all time the age-old jockeying for world power and prestige which was believed to be the cause of war. With the defeat of the "aggressors" there would never again be need for nation to fear nation and the world could once more take up the tasks of peace which were the sincere desire of all peoples, as political leaders in both Europe and America continually assured their citizens and each other.

But events of the past few years produced drastic changes in this picture of optimism. The power struggle between the Soviet Union and the United States has created fear and dissension among most nations of the world, and has produced unforeseen complications in the United Nations organization itself. To American supporters of the United Nations idea these complications have been wholly incomprehensible. They see the countries who have benefited most from American economic and political assistance voting against us in the UN; traditional allies and friends openly charging that the United States is "warmongering"; small nations denouncing us as "imperialistic." The situation is one which is producing profound disillusionment in the American people, who are still not too well informed as to the exact nature of the responsibilities which they have assumed in the world arena.

This disillusionment became even more pronounced in the early part of 1952 when the political campaign got under way. And although support of the UN remains a cardinal principle of American foreign policy, in various quarters questions are being asked about American participation in the UN, questions which may lead to major changes in our foreign policy.

That there has been a change of attitude on the part of the American people has become increasingly evident. In Congress, for example, in 1946 and 1947 UN support was overwhelming. In 1948 and 1949, the veto problem created a desire to "strengthen the UN" and a number of bills were introduced and committee hearings were held with this end in view. Then in 1950, with the Korean War and the signing of the North Atlantic Treaty, emphasis shifted toward the creation of an alliance of the Atlantic nations even though nominally "within the framework of the UN." By 1951 bills were being introduced calling for withdrawal from the UN or modification of certain features of the UN machinery, with even greater emphasis on regional organization. Active opposition to UN policies in 1952 was expressed by a small group of Republican Senators up for reelection, including John Bricker of Ohio and James P. Kem of Missouri.

Other straws in the wind also could be noted. After World War II ended, twenty-three states put themselves on record favoring some form of world government, even going beyond the UN as presently constituted. Some twenty senators and a hundred representatives in Congress publicly favored such an idea and a federal world government movement spread rapidly. But by the end of 1951, seventeen of these states had rescinded their world government resolutions. On UN Day—October 24, 1951 —display of the UN flag was objected to by patriotic organizations in a number of local communities, sometimes violently. Since that time, the Daughters of the American Revolution, the Veterans of Foreign Wars, and other patriotic organizations have taken official action denouncing various UN activities, in particular objecting to "propagandizing" by the United Nations Educational, Social, and Cultural Organization in the schools of America, the teaching about UNESCO and the UN, and the use of materials published by either organization as part of classroom studies.

These and other developments point to the existence of considerable controversy over American participation in the United Nations, a controversy which seems to center around three main points:

1. *The ability of the UN to "keep the peace."* Much of expressed public resentment directed at the UN stems from the failure to prevent, and later to "stop," the Korean conflict. There has been considerable discussion, pro and con, as to whether the UN was ever intended to be a "cure" for war— and if it was not, what it was intended to do. This question has been serious enough to be given consideration by Trygve Lie, president of the UN, and by members of the American delegation, who have made frequent speeches explaining the values of the UN and what it can be expected to accomplish.

2. *The status of the Constitution under the UN.* This is a major point of controversy with lawyers and journalists, in particular. It centers upon the question of whether UN de-

cisions may directly affect domestic laws. Chief figure in this dispute is Senator Bricker who charges that the UN Human Rights Covenant, still unsigned by the United States, would violate Constitutional rights of free press, free speech, and freedom of religion. The gist of his argument is that the First Amendment specifies that Congress can pass no laws abridging these freedoms, yet by virtue of a "treaty', such as this UN agreement, UN "law" would be substituted for American law. In particular, he points to the provisions of the Human Rights Covenant which permit certain restrictions on freedom of informational exchanges as may be needed for "protection of national security, public order, safety, health or morals, or the protection of the rights and freedom of others" and exclusion of the press from criminal trials—a "right" which the American press holds extremely important. His alarm stems from the decision of a California court that the UN Covenant was the "highest authority," and even though this was later tempered by the Supreme Court of California, Senator Bricker holds that the problem involved presents a threat to our freedoms and must be decided before we become involved any further in international organizations. Specifically, he would want to know just how far we wish to go in subordinating our rights and privileges under the Constitution to the decisions of a majority of nations in the UN, including the Soviet Union and its satellites.

3. *The economics of international cooperation.* This point actually consists of three problems. The first is the dispute over the relative share of financial support being contributed by member nations in the UN. There have been many charges that the United States is having to carry too much of the load. A second problem relates to the burden of foreign aid on the American taxpayer. Senator Tom Connally, the Administration foreign policy spokesman, charged that America couldn't support the world forever and that some limitation on foreign aid was going to have to be made. The third problem has had little popular discussion, since it concerns foreign trade and the type of international trade agreements which should be adopted. Various economists and businessmen have debated the question, and it seems

to be one of the main sources of foreign distrust of the good faith of the United States.

All of these add up to lessened enthusiasm for the UN (and for international organization generally) in the United States. The blame can be placed on a combination of factors: the continuing stalemate in Korea, growing military expenditures, unpopularity of the draft, rising prices and inflation, plus higher taxes. While sentiment still appears generally favorable to the UN, there is a strong tendency to be much more critical of specific programs and policies. There is a much stronger demand for results, for greater effectiveness, and a general impatience with delays and lack of progress.

The whole problem of international organization and our participation in the UN is under review. Should American participation in the UN be limited in some manner, should we look outside the UN for other and perhaps more effective means of advancing American foreign policy, or should we abandon the world organization altogether? In brief, What kind of international organization should the United States support?

Before approaching this problem, it seems important to examine the situation in which we find ourselves today.

THE UN UNDER FIRE [1]

Although the United Nations is just an innocent bystander, delegates and officials are beginning to realize that the organization will be the target of many a brickbat before the United States elections are over. Ignorance rather than malice appears to be the basic reason for some of the attacks, but they come at a time when the prestige of the United Nations, both in the United States and elsewhere, has dropped as a result of the failure to reach an armistice in Korea.

Moreover, since the Security Council is paralyzed by the Soviet veto, the free world is being forced to rely upon such

[1] From "UN Is Facing Mounting Criticism in the U.S." by Thomas J. Hamilton, New York *Times* UN correspondent. New York *Times*. p E5. June 8, 1952. Reprinted by permission.

regional organizations as NATO rather than the United Nations for protection against any new Communist aggression.

The current attacks on the organization in this country are attributed in part to dissatisfaction with the Korean situation. Senator Taft has denounced American participation in the United Nations action in Korea as "Truman's War."

However, the basic reason, according to persons . . . in close touch with the situation, is simply that the isolationist wing of the Republican party has started an offensive against both the Truman Administration and those Republicans . . . who favor international cooperation. The United Nations, whose very presence in the United States is a symbol of such a policy, can hardly be expected to keep out of the line of fire.

Such attacks increased in volume and intensity as a result of a court decision in California. The ruling struck down the state's law against purchase of land by Japanese on the ground that this was contrary to the United Nations Charter . . . The decision aroused fears that both the Charter and agreements reached subsequently under the United Nations . . . would be used to impose fundamental changes in state as well as federal law. Fifty-six senators, led by John W. Bricker, Mr. Taft's Ohio colleague, took the decision so seriously that they introduced a resolution to prevent such action in the future by amending the United States Constitution. . . . The decision was set aside by the California State Supreme Court, which declared that the land law was illegal, not because of the Charter, but because it was contrary to the Fourteenth Amendment. The court pointed out that the nondiscriminatory provisions in the United Nations Charter were not intended to be self-executing. . . . If and when the United States Government wanted to make them legally enforceable, it would have to enact separate legislation.

The original decision, however, was widely publicized, and so was a fantastic claim that United Nations troops had "occupied" four cities in southern California and were on the point of threatening homes and firesides throughout the country. The Daughters of the American Revolution meanwhile became apprehensive about the United Nations because they heard, equally mistakenly, that Admiral Lynde D. McCormick, commander of NATO naval forces in the Atlantic, was flying the United Nations flag alongside that of the United States in his headquarters at Norfolk. Actually, the "occupation" of the California cities was simply an exercise by civil government units of the United States Army, who, as members of the United Nations forces, were testing their preparations to take over Korean towns. And it was the NATO flag, not the United Nations flag, that Admiral Mc-Cormick was flying.

Whether the truth will ever catch up with such ill-founded charges is another matter. The situation is the more serious because of another recent development, the repeated charges that a number of American Communists are on the United Nations payroll. . . . Fears concerning Communist espionage are so widespread that this situation hardly strengthens the position of the United Nations in this country. It is to be hoped that this issue will not cause any lasting damage to the standing of the organization in the United States. More troubles are ahead, for the United States, which until now has been on the winning side on practically all important issues before the United Nations, is beginning to lose what Soviet delegates like to call its "mechanical majority."

Primarily as a result of a United States abstention, the Security Council recently failed to place the Tunisian question on its agenda, but it appears certain that the General Assembly will do so this fall, whether the United States approves or not. In the General Assembly last winter the Arab and Asiatic delegates, with the assistance of some Latin American representatives, passed a resolution over United States opposition which is intended to prepare the way for a huge international fund to finance the development of backward countries. . . . It is clear that the [Economic and Social] Council will go ahead with the preliminary steps involved in setting up the fund—which, as the underdeveloped countries see it, should be contributed by the United States virtually 100 per cent.

Meanwhile the Human Rights Commission, again over the opposition of the United States, has been giving such an anticolonial, antiforeign investments flavor to a proposed covenant on economic and social rights that the United States will probably refuse to sign it. Similarly, the United States, which played a leading part in drawing up conventions on news gathering and freedom of information, objects so strongly to certain provisions that it proposed . . . that the whole project be dropped. Regardless of the correctness or otherwise of United States policy on these issues, the point is that if any considerable number of Assembly votes go against the United States, American isolationists will find new grounds for attacks on the United Nations. The opening of the Assembly is being postponed until shortly before the United States elections, but those studying the question are more concerned with the long-range effects. . . . United Nations officials concede that the organization is going through a difficult period, but they believe that as far as the United States is concerned, the current attacks will die off after the election. There will still remain the arduous task of making the organization work effectively despite great power differences, but they hope that with time even this can be achieved.

KOREA AND COLLECTIVE SECURITY [2]

The one year of heavy fighting and one year of heavy haggling in Korea have changed the shape of our world. The impact of Korea upon military developments and national armaments has been profound and the intensification of the two-world conflict, and the realignment of world power that have taken place in the past two years were in major part a result of the Korean war. . . . It has put into the field for the first time a United Nations force composed of contingents from sixteen countries; it speeded the activation of NATO, and it has helped to expedite the beginning of the renaissance of Germany and Japan as great powers. The historical repercussions of Korea are still influencing our times; indeed, future historians may record Korea as a turning point. But where the

[2] From "A World Balance Sheet: Two Years After the Attack in Korea," by Hanson W. Baldwin, New York *Times* military editor. New York *Times*. p E5. June 22, 1952. Reprinted by permission.

road may lead and how the final balance sheet will add up, no man can tell. . . .

The United States intervention in the Korean war prevented the conquest of Southern Korea by communism and has altered and delayed the Communist timetable for the conquest of Asia. The concentration of enemy strength in Korea and the simultaneous United States aid to Indo-China and Formosa—a direct result of our Korean intervention—probably prevented the conquest of these two areas by the Chinese Communists. The psychological and political effect of the United States intervention was initially magical; Communist aggression was openly challenged and hurled back, anticommunism was encouraged everywhere. The United Nations support and the dispatch of troops and units from sixteen countries to fight in a common cause against a common enemy initially strengthened the United Nations, and hurt Soviet Russia. The Inchon landing—and later— the hard-fought victories of General Ridgway and General Van Fleet restored confidence, shaken by early reverses, in the effectiveness of United States military power.

United States rearmament was a direct result of Korea. The armed services today are several times larger and many times more powerful and effective than they were in June 1950, and the productive base of the United States military industrial effort —though still far from producing to capacity—is broader than it was two years ago. Many weaknesses in military policy and industrial mobilization have been remedied.

Korea spurred collective security arrangements all over the world. The Japanese peace treaty and the various Pacific security arrangements, which may lead to a Pacific pact, were expedited as a direct result of Korea. . . .

In Europe, the nations of the North Atlantic Treaty Organization, stirred and shaken by the open aggression in Korea and the demonstrated power of satellite puppet armies, shifted their emphasis to armament and—despite delays, disappointments and hesitations—have banded together into a military coalition which is considerably more effective than the disparate and disorganized national forces of two years ago. The European Army treaty and the Bonn peace agreement with West Germany have been signed (though not ratified); Turkey and Greece have been included in the NATO grouping and Yugoslavia, once isolated, naked and vulnerable, has been assisted with military supplies and moral support.

The blatant nature of the Communist assault in Korea and the demonstrated determination and ability of the United States to oppose it have heartened anti-Communist forces everywhere.

The entries in red ink are large. We have, so far, held South Korea at the price of great expense, large casualties and the devastation of all of Korea. But Korea's geographical position—part of the mainland of Asia, close to two great powers, Communist China and Communist Russia—make any long-term security for South Korea a major problem.

We are fighting a war in Korea in an area of the world where no decision can possibly be reached against the main enemy—Soviet Russia. We are fighting largely on the enemy's terms in a region where he can bring to bear his great numerical superiority in manpower. The United States has committed to Korea a sizable portion of its active military strength . . . whereas Soviet Russia has freedom of action and is opposing us largely with her satellite forces.

Since its intervention in Korea, Communist China has consolidated its grip upon the mainland, and with the material help of Soviet Russia has become stronger—not weaker—both in Korea and in China proper. . . . We may be witnessing a process of peculiar and tremendous historical significance to our times— the beginning of the growth of China as a modern military power. Moreover, Korea has been carefully tied in to Communist global war plans. Continuation of the war in Korea has forced dispersion of United States and United Nations forces and has siphoned military aid from Europe to the Orient. We are, as yet, really strong nowhere; a great vacuum of power exists in the Middle East, and United States and Allied rearmament has been answered with increased satellite and Russian armament. The European Army still exists only on paper; the Western German zone's rearmament is but a dream, and numerous Soviet delaying actions—with the threat of an Eastern zone army (already in being in cadre form) as the ultimate—will undoubtedly postpone the creation in Western Europe of an effective military force. The answer to the question, who gains by time, is problematical and the Soviet Union, with the help of Communist parties everywhere, is still creating political and psychological dissensions and is forcing the United States and its allies to expend huge sums for, as yet, indecisive gains.

Russia has, moreover, capitalized upon our mistakes and weaknesses. Her psychological warfare has made headway as a result of some of our mistakes at Panmunjom, and the inept handling of prisoners of war at Koje Island. She has charged us, with complete falsity but nevertheless some effectiveness, with germ warfare. And . . . we are still tied down to a limited war of attrition—a stalemated war—in Korea, with no end in sight.

All of this has led to perhaps the most serious debit in the Korean ledger. The people of the nation, frustrated and confused and divided in an election year, are split and unhappy and groping. And the normal schisms of a coalition have been worsened by time, the lack of decisive progress in winning either a peace or a war in Korea, and by the differences between ourselves and our allies about Asiatic policies. The Western and United Nations coalitions have suffered these last few months.

EUROPEAN FEARS OF AMERICAN FOREIGN POLICY [3]

A good many people are beginning to speculate about just how wise, adroit and farsighted American foreign policy is. Europe depends on us but this does not mean that there is blind faith in our diplomatic perception. We happen to be the strong boys of a coalition. Just because at this moment we have four United States ambassadors and five ministers assigned to Paris our Allies are not overwhelmed with the logic of the arguments presented by Washington. . . . [The] Continent recalls a paucity of long-range American political conceptions

[3] From "Europe Asks Questions on U.S. Foreign Policy," by C. L. Sulzberger, New York *Times* chief foreign correspondent. New York *Times*. p E3. May 11, 1952.

during World War II. It is felt that we fought the war to win it—but did not give sufficient attention to the job of establishing the peace which must follow. Strictly military considerations affected our thinking on such problems as a possible Balkans campaign or the urging of a Soviet attack on atrophied Japan. The limitations of such a policy have been made obvious by history. Now some of our friends wonder whether we may not be fighting the "cold war" with the same sort of short-range and inadequate goals as the "hot" one.

Success in the recent conflict automatically created vacuums in Europe and Asia by destroying Germany and Japan. But what were the political preparations to shore up two boneless continents? . . . As far as can be detected here there were no alternative American policies prepared in advance. Indeed, there is a vast admiration for the brilliant improvisations of the Truman Doctrine, Marshall Plan and Korean defense scheme. But . . . [the] Continent does not want to gamble any more than it has to on improvising.

It saw in the past the loss of Eastern Europe without even an effort by the American-led Allies to offer any other political alternative to that region than either communism or a prewar status quo.

What are we ready for now? For example, a singularly wise statesman said just the other day that he had been informed that we could have a revolution any day we desired in a certain Soviet satellite but "we simply wouldn't know what to do with it." What are our plans if, trying to restore the balance of power by using revisionist-minded Germany and Japan, their aspirations lead abruptly into the Soviet heartland? There are many who would like to know how we expect to handle situations which our own policy may create five years hence.

Of course, while such European nations as France and Britain are vastly interested in Asia, where they have their own private wars to fight in addition to helping out in the Korean affair, they are naturally primarily concerned with American policy . . . in the West. The military, economic and, indeed, political defenses of . . . [the] Continent are openly predicated upon the assumption that Germany, or at least that portion included in the Bonn Federal Republic, can be rearmed and integrated in the framework of the democratic coalition. Occidental leaders have frequently stated that Europe simply cannot be protected without German aid.

Planning has proceeded on that assumption. The project for a European Defense Community including Germany . . . soon . . . will be signed. However, between the signature of a treaty and its implementation by parliamentary ratification looms a political Grand Canyon. Chancellor Konrad Adenauer, strongest German supporter of the project, has been losing popular support steadily during the past few month. We have put all our eggs in his basket. We have managed not only to ignore but even to affront his most powerful opponent, Kurt Schumacher, the Socialist leader, and should the venerable Adenauer die or be defeated, the entire project, which we publicly admit is the key to Western defense would probably collapse.

Just what do we do if we cannot have Germany? Is it true that we cannot hold the West without Bonn's active aid? Even so, is it judicious to say so? Declarations to this effect have had the obvious logical repercussions. They incite Moscow to do everything in its considerable power to bribe the Germans away from the West. They prompt the Germans themselves to keep raising the price of collaboration.

If Germany is ultimately going to join with the rest of free Europe, what will its final asking price be? The Germans are now harping upon our pledge that they shall be treated as equals. Will the equality be relative? How will the Occident rationalize, for example, French control of the Saar, ethnographically a Teutonic area? There are some European statesmen who are saying privately nowadays that in our German dealings we have made the mistake of placing the cart of integration before the horse of unification. One may not like it, but the Germans, just like the Koreans, want their country reunited. Many of them, perhaps more emotional than intellectual, might even be prepared to risk taking their chances with Soviet domination of a unified homeland rather than gamble with indefinite truncation.

There are many Europeans who would like to see some American spokesman emerge with a clear statement of an alternative defense policy and an alternative Germany policy if the proposed European community does not materialize. There are those who wonder if we do not tend to trap ourselves by saying "No" automatically every time the Kremlin says "Yes," without considering the consequences—just the way Moscow pulled a serious boner in spurning the Marshall Plan.

A good many businessmen in both Europe and Asia are speculating about the duration of the present politically imposed economic blockade. Just how long, for example, can Japan refuse to buy Soviet coal at one third the price offered in the United States or refrain from selling textiles to Communist China? Do the magnates of the Ruhr contemplate with equanimity the loss of traditional Balkan markets? And anyway, can the technocrat democracies of the West ignore indefinitely such Iron Curtain raw materials as manganese and monazite sands?

Europe is grateful for the aid and confidence of the United States. It recognizes the force and power of America. But it prays for farseeing wisdom in the political leadership which has been thrust upon us by historical circumstance.

THE STATUS OF AMERICAN FOREIGN
POLICY IN 1952 [4]

There's no doubt that the United States has moved fast and far since the Chinese Communists intervened in Korea in the fall of 1950. You can see this as clearly in the evolution of the containment policy itself as in the growth of American military power. The Truman Doctrine of 1947, the beginning of containment, called for temporary assistance to individual countries that were threatened by Russian aggression. But after the Chinese Reds marched into Korea, the United States began organizing a long-term world alliance of non-Communist countries. A Pacific defense pact was added to the Atlantic alliance, and a start was made on a Middle East defense system.

[4] From "Foreign Policy: U.S. Takes a New Road," news story. *Business Week.* p 101-4. January 5, 1952. Reprinted by permission.

This kind of global policy is a tremendous step for a country that operated under a neutrality act hardly more than a decade ago. Moreover, the United States has gone beyond the traditional alliances of the 19th century, which Americans so long damned as "entanglements." We're engaged now in an effort to integrate the entire democratic world, even though that encroaches on our traditional ideas of national sovereignty.

Developments abroad paralleled, at least roughly, change on the home front. Foreign policy today has a priority that it's never had before except in World War II. You can see that in the national feeling that the future of the United States depends on events abroad and in the broad agreement that we can't avoid world-wide commitments. You can see it, too, in the tighter integration of the branches of the Federal Government that deal with foreign policy.

The National Security Council, for instance, has become almost a political general staff. From it the President gets the joint advice of the State, Defense, and Treasury departments, plus the Chiefs of Staff. A separate body, the Mutual Security Administration, handles the financial side of our global policy. A central intelligence organization (CIA) coordinates all foreign intelligence data. And we now have a division of psychological warfare, the first in our peacetime history.

There is no historical parallel to the overnight revolution in the scope of United States foreign policy and in the mechanics of policy making. The world powers of the past had a century or more to learn the game of power politics.

Take what's happened to the State Department in the past quarter century. . . . Even in the late twenties, State was a revenue producer in some year (via visa fees, etc.) rather than a colossal spender of public funds. Its relations with Congress were relatively simple. Only the occasional congressman took much interest in our foreign affairs, and only the Senate, with its treaty-making powers, got really involved. . . . But there's no longer the leisurely atmosphere of old. And the department that fathered the Marshall Plan and the Atlantic alliance has Congress on its neck almost from day to day. For foreign policy making on the Hill is now being done as much by the cost-conscious House Appropriations Committee as by the Senate and House Foreign Affairs Committees.

As Congress takes a bigger and bigger part in foreign affairs, the balances of the United States constitutional setup make the formulation and execution of foreign policy more and more difficult for the Administration. By comparison with Britain, not to mention Soviet Russia, any United States administration is seriously hamstrung in making big or fast decisions. This constitutional difficulty has been aggravated under the Truman Administration by the bad blood between Congress and the White House, and by the suspicions directed at the State Department.

Even within the Administration itself, making policy has become a complicated process. Smoother functioning of the National Security Council hasn't solved the problem of getting decisions through Washington's huge bureaucracy. For one thing, State has grown to a size where its policy ideas often have to be reached by negotiation among the department's regional divisions. Then, on big issues, the conflicting views of [the departments of] State, Defense, Treasury, and the Mutual Security Administration have to be ironed out. Unless the President makes foreign policy, as Roosevelt did, quick and bold decisions are hard to get under a system like this.

For example, it is clear that, with only a few exceptions, the nation state is becoming an anachronism in the mid-twentieth century. The United States and Russia still have the resources to function effectively as single national units. That's no longer true of the countries of Western Europe. Some form of supernational organization—perhaps a confederation—is essential if Western Europe is to survive as a power center. But it has taken several years to get Washington bureaucracy to accept an idea like this; it still isn't part of Washington's working philosophy.

It isn't just the mechanics of policy making that act as a brake on foreign policy. The United States is handicapped by peculiarly American attitudes that grow out of our great wealth and relative self-sufficiency.

Unlike the other world powers, the United States is a satisfied nation, has been for fifty years. It has no territorial ambitions and no critical economic needs to be satisfied by control over foreign countries. Thus the dynamic factor in our policy is the search for peace and the maintenance of the status quo. This doesn't lead to the kind of long-term planning and tough realism that went into the making of Britain's foreign policy through the centuries.

In theory, this approach should make it easy for the United States to give the democratic world a strong moral and political lead. But in fact it doesn't. One reason is the huge gap between our wealth and that of our allies. Another is that most of the rest of the world regards the United States, no less than Russia, as out of step with the twentieth century trend toward democratic socialism.

Paradoxically, the tendency of the American people and Congress to take a "moralistic slant" on foreign affairs hampers our leadership, too. Take the Kem Amendment to the Mutual Security Act, which aims at cutting Western Europe's trade with Russia and its satellites. The majority in Congress looked at this in strictly black and white terms. The United States doesn't trade with the Communists; so why should the allies to whom we give aid? If rigidly applied, the Kem Amendment would weaken rather than strengthen our NATO allies.

These limitations on a smoothly functioning foreign policy haven't kept the United States from holding the democratic world together in the past five years. But in the months ahead they could stymie United States policy at critical points, perhaps give Russia openings it shouldn't get. You can see the dangers if you look at the problems we face in several critical spots.

(1) *The Middle East*—The old order in this area is disappearing fast. And the British aren't strong enough to midwife a new order. Only the United States can do this job. But to do it quickly, Washington would have to use the kind of power tactics that Americans have long frowned on. Also it would mean long-term political, financial, and military commitment. Given our constitutional setup, no United States administration could get away with either until Congress and the people are

sold on the necessity of preventing a power vacuum in this area.

(2) *Western Europe*—Friction between the United States and Western Europe is likely to grow this year. On the one hand, many Europeans are seriously questioning the United States leadership of the Western alliance. They say the United States pushed rearmament too fast, underestimated its impact on the European economics. We aggravated the problem first by stockpiling frantically and then by slashing purchases of such big dollar earners as Malayan tin. On this side of the Atlantic, Congress is in a mood to be tough on Europe—for its failure to (1) boost coal output, and (2) get ahead with economic and political unification. If this mood produces a cut in aid, or drastic new conditions, United States-European relations could deteriorate rapidly.

(3) *Britain*—The British are considered our last ditch allies. Yet it's now clear to unofficial experts here and abroad that the foundations of British strength have crumbled so much that, in a period of world tension, some new way must be found to maintain British strength. It's probable that either a modified lend-lease system or some kind of economic integration between the United States and the British Commonwealth is needed to do the job. There's no sign of this kind of approach in Washington today. On the contrary, although the present British crisis was foreseen in Washington . . . the Administration has made no real moves to ease the crisis, let alone solve it.

(4) *Asia*—The United States has halted Communist aggression in Korea. But all the gains from the fighting haven't been on our side. The Korean war has consolidated Mao Tse-tung's position in mainland China and cemented the Moscow-Peiping alliance. Most of our friends in the United Nations want the United States to accept Communist China as a *fait accompli* and drop our "moralistic" attitude toward the new regime. What's more, they are inclined to let Peiping have Formosa.

Add things up, and you get this picture of American foreign policy at the turn of the year [January 1952]: The United States already had grown into a world colossus far faster than any country in history. A constitution and traditions based on safe seclusion so far haven't kept us from adjusting almost overnight to a new role in the world.

AMERICAN INVOLVEMENT IN INTERNATIONAL AFFAIRS

EDITOR'S INTRODUCTION

So much has happened in the world in the past few years that it is almost impossible for any one individual to be "fully informed." This is especially true, even in Congress, with respect to the details of American involvement in foreign affairs. And general knowledge of the extent of our foreign commitments is limited, for the most part, to a handful of major treaties (such as the North Atlantic Pact) and such large-scale operations as the Marshall Plan or the Point Four Program.

Except for the broad outlines of these measures, most people have no idea what is involved in terms of organization, personnel and financial details. While it is easy enough to talk about American participation in the United Nations, what does this mean in numbers of additional employees in the State Department, additional offices and ministers abroad, additional problems and headaches for other governmental agencies? Only through the slow process of trial and error are Americans discovering methods of operating "internationally" and learning how to cope with the countless problems of world leadership.

We speak in such high-sounding terms as "implementing" a treaty. And we rarely think that this word "implementing" means the actual down-to-earth details of making the particular program work. In a foreign aid program it means getting together a staff of trained people; setting up offices and commissions everywhere that the program is going to operate: purchasing commissions to secure the supplies, investigating commissions to insure that our aid is efficiently and fairly distributed, bookkeeping departments, payroll and personnel units, and the countless other procedural operations necessary to efficient management.

An interesting and not too well-known sidelight on the effects of United States participation in international organizations is the number of changes which such participation has brought about in the American government itself. Such developments were outlined recently by H. Field Haviland, Jr., of Haverford College, in an article in *Current History* (January 1952), in which he remarked that of the fifty-nine major departments and agencies "approximately" forty-six of these play some part in the international drama.

Within the State Department, for example, there is now a Bureau of United Nations Affairs which has within its jurisdiction a United Nations Planning Staff, a Refugees and Displaced Persons Staff, an Office of United Nations Political and Security Affairs, an Office of United Nations Economic and Social Affairs, an Office of Dependent Area Affairs, and an Office of International Administration and Conferences. And outside the Bureau most of the other State Department units, says Professor Haviland, have a "United Nations Adviser," and have frequent contact with UN affairs.

One notable result of the "multitude of UN activities" has been that a very large number of governmental agencies and bureaus, normally not concerned with foreign policy, have been directly affected and have had to develop liaison relationships with the Department of State (and often the UN itself) to enable American policy to have some element of coordination. The device most frequently used to work out interdepartmental relationships for this purpose is the inter-agency committee; Professor Haviland says there are approximately thirty such committees in which the Department of State currently participates.

The process of conversion from a relatively isolationist continental power to the position of world leadership has produced untold complications and much unnecessary duplication of activities. These are natural consequences of expansion. But to profit by experience requires some understanding at least of what problems we have faced and are facing now in this new international position of the United States.

Before attempting to reach conclusions as to the merits or drawbacks of a particular proposal, before saying, "Yes, let's join a world federation" or "Let's get out of the United Nations while we can," we ought to examine in brief outline some of the things we are now doing in the world, see how far we are committed and understand the implications of either sudden withdrawal or sudden change in the present trend. Especially should it be remembered that treaties are promises between nations and that United States policy is based on a moral principle that this country never breaks a promise. For this reason then is it important to know how many promises we have made abroad before deciding what we *ought* to do.

ESSENTIALS OF UNITED STATES FOREIGN POLICY [1]

The program of the American people is designed . . . to provide mutual security through common effort to avert aggression or to halt aggression if it cannot be averted.

The American program for peace encompasses: first, active participation in the United Nations; second, regional security arrangements within the framework of the United Nations— like the North Atlantic Treaty and the Organization of American States; third, military assistance programs by which we furnish military aid to increase the strength of friendly nations and thus strengthen the defenses of the free world; fourth, economic assistance programs to aid certain friendly nations to stand on their own two feet in areas where human welfare is the first essential in the struggle against communism. . . .

This program is so vast that it challenges the imagination and wisdom of all of us, but upon it rests the hopes of the world; and we must make it work. . . . Out of the chaos of World War II rose the concept of the United Nations. It envisaged the creation of a world instrument capable at least of giving to all its members security against aggression. Of course, it is imperfect but still there is no better instrument at hand for preventing another world war. It has been rent by the challenge of a counterfeit philosophy which purports to offer freedom but which is really based upon slavery and the complete sub-

[1] From "Duty, Honor, Country," address delivered at West Point, March 16, 1952, by General J. Lawton Collins, Chief of Staff, United States Army. *Vital Speeches of the Day.* 18:368-70. April 1, 1952. Reprinted by permission.

jugation of the individual to the state. The free world, holding the dignity of the individual to be supreme and seeing the gulf widen, found it necessary to meet the challenge by adopting additional security measures.

The North Atlantic Treaty Organization is one of these measures, and in it lies a tangible assurance of collective strength which can deter an aggressor from launching war. The security of Western Europe is vital to the security of the United States, and the defense of it is, in effect, a defense of the United States—a factor which . . . is often overlooked.

IMPLICATIONS OF WORLD LEADERSHIP [2]

You are, at the beginning of A.D. 1952, committed by treaty to defend thirty-seven nations. By the presence of American troops, or the promises of United States leaders, you are effectively committed to defend five more. And though your government has not announced it, it is commonly assumed that you would defend nine or ten other countries (as well as most of the colonies) of the non-Soviet world. Through your representatives in Congress you still reserve the constitutional power to declare, or not to declare, war. But this is a power so altered by Stalin and technology as to be almost no power at all. . . .

How and why his staggering commitments came to rest on the United States citizen is a much told story. Yet so rapidly have the commitments been assumed, and in such bewildering variety, that the citizen has scarcely sensed the full extent of his involvement. . . .

Most of the great empires of history were centuries in the building, centuries in authority, centuries in decay. The United States, from what was practically a standing start in 1939, by 1945 had marshaled a military force incomparably stronger than any other the world had known. Then, with recklessness equally unique, the United States proceeded to scrap this force in a bare twelve months. But shortly even that was to be reversed, and the United States set about redeeming its misjudgment, first with

[2] From "The Cost of Being an American," editorial. *Fortune.* 45:53-4. January 1952. Reprinted by permission.

diplomacy and money, later with men and arms as well. Much of
the diplomacy has been fumbling, some of the money has been ill
spent, the rearmament has often seemed maddeningly slow. But
. . . the American people have compressed an extraordinary
amount of history into the past five years.

The power and responsibility are infernally expensive. The
United States citizen has become the underwriter of foreign
solvencies as well as sovereignties. He has never acknowledged
such a commitment in so many words, but the foreign belief
in it is scarcely surprising.

In the six years ending last June 30, the United States made
foreign grants of $22,343,812,162. It made foreign loans
totaling $10,862,223,305, some of them disguised as gifts, not
many of them exactly bankable. It put up $3,385,000,000 of the
capitalization for the World Bank and Monetary fund. Grand
total: $36,591,035,467.

For the current fiscal year, ending next June 30, the United
States will probably spend $2 billion for foreign economic aid.
It will probably spend $48 billion on the United States armed
forces, and those of our allies, and on atomic energy, stockpiling, and other programs directly contributing to United States
military strength—to our ability to back up our world-wide commitments. Adding to these sums the cost of the Veterans Administration and servicing of the national debt (which is largely
chargeable to our part in World War II), it can be said that
America's relations with the rest of the world, bad and good,
account for 87 per cent of the $70-billion Federal budget.

To bring all this down from rarefied billions to the figures
that really hurt, one reckoning of the cost of being an American
is simply the per capita share of the 1952 defense budget—$400,
or approximately $1,500 per family. . . .

The nations taking our dollars and our guarantees do not
rejoice in the relationship. The London *Economist* was com-
plaining not long ago of the automatic majority commanded by
the United States in the directorate of the International Monetary
Fund. . . . "You'll never be popular," a distinguished European
recently advised some American friends. "Nobody will thank
you, and nobody will like you."

It is of no special importance whether [they] . . . love us . . . so long as they are sufficiently devoted to their own countries to defend them, and sufficiently informed to recognize their enemies. A great deal of waste motion is introduced into United States foreign policy and information programs by a hankering after a kind of international affection that simply doesn't exist. But if America's strength is grating to our allies, it is sometimes alarming to the American. It can also make him feel gullible, or guilty, or just plain embarrassed. . . .

The first reason is obvious: Americans are profoundly reluctant to think of themselves as an imperial people. We fail, happily, by the first test of empire. We give, we advise, we influence, we guarantee. But we do not govern. . . .

The simple fact is that the United States is not attempting to impose an American empire. What the Americans have is a Proposition, not an empire—a proposition whose principles have universal application for the betterment of mankind. The American Commitment is imposed on us—by our own ideals, wealth, and strength, and by the instability and weakness that lie between us and the power of the Soviet Union.

The United States cannot play the divisive game of the Balance of Power. That was a natural enough game for a great sea power, more or less immune from invasion, in a world of six or seven "great powers." It is not a game open to the United States today. In one decade all the "great powers" have been destroyed, or have declined to lower rank—save two, the USSR and the United States of America.

In this rarest of historical situations there can be no hard-and-fast defensive "loops" or "cordons" or "lines"—except one that goes around the world, no more than a line on paper. There can be only patterns of strength and of principles. The pattern of strength of the American is regaining; coherent patterns of principles are yet to be discerned in the policies of our present leadership. . . .

Many European statesmen privately urge the United States to "meddle" more in the internal affairs of the ECA [Economic Cooperation Administration] countries. Americans have made all too little use of the bargaining power—in behalf of economic opportunity and military security—that the numerous aid programs should have provided. But if the United States "interferes" in the internal politics of other countries, many Americans will object, what difference is there between that and the Soviet policy? Just the difference between the United States of America and the USSR.

There is not going to be any happy morning when the American wakes up and finds his world-wide problems have gone away. Should the problems disappear, it would probably mean . . . that United States power had disappeared. In *The Pattern of Imperialism*, Professor E. M. Winslow wrote of the growth of Rome and the other Mediterranean empires: "The choice . . . in classic times," was between "exercising power yourself and having it exercised against you." In these unclassic times, that is again the choice.

RECORD OF FOREIGN AID: WAR AND POSTWAR
THROUGH DECEMBER 31, 1951 [3]

Investments in: (in millions)

International Monetary Fund	$2,750
International Bank for Reconstruction and Development	635

Grants utilized:

Lend-lease	48,674
Mutual security:	
economic and technical assistance	10,717
military aid	2,046
Civilian supplies	6,252
UNRRA	2,671
Post-UNRRA	299
Interim aid	556
Philippine rehabilitation	631
Chinese stabilization	500

[3] From remarks by Senator William Langer, Republican of North Dakota, before the Senate, during debate on the Mutual Defense appropriation bill. *Congressional Record*. 98:4570. April 28, 1952.

Grants utilized—*Continued*

Chinese military aid	123
Refugee assistance	288
International children's emergency fund	81
Inter-American aid	89
American Red Cross	73
Other grants	225

Credits utilized:

Special British loan	3,750
Export-Import Bank	3,266
Surplus property (incl. merchant ships)	1,338
Credit agreement offsets to grants	1,256
Lend-lease (excl. settlement credit)	418
Mutual security (incl. loans to Spain and India)	1,277
Other	863

> * Gross foreign aid and capital in-
> vestment $88,180

* Includes all aid under the Mutual Security Act of 1951, Mutual Defense Assistance Act of 1949, the Economic Cooperation Act of 1948, all aid except military under China Aid Act of 1948, and assistance to Korea by ECA; does not include Greek-Turkish assistance under Public Law 75 prior to the MDAA of 1948. Source: Clearing Office for Foreign Transactions, Office of Business Economics, United States Department of Commerce.

FINANCING TECHNICAL DEVELOPMENT: POINT FOUR PROGRAM [4]

Point Four has become a settled part of American foreign policy. And although the program is young, it is already apparent that Point Four is a success. . . .

Under the Point Four program, we now have 619 American technicians serving in 34 countries, and there are 372 people from other countries studying techniques here in the United

[4] From "What Is Point Four?" address by Secretary of State Dean Acheson before the Americans for Democratic Action, New York City, January 25, 1952. *United States Department of State Bulletin.* 26:155-9. February 4, 1952.

States. All told, there are some 216 Point Four projects under way in Latin America, Africa, the Middle East, and Asia. And side by side with these are many other technical-cooperation projects being carried on by the United Nations, and by other agencies of our government. . . .

These Point Four activities have a new significance, which makes them more than unrelated good deeds. Under the Point Four Program, these activities are but the first steps in a process that can change—and is changing—the whole aspect of life in these areas . . . that is what makes it an important part of our foreign policy today.

For example, the work . . . in one small area in northern India—not more than a hundred square miles in size—has been followed by an agreement with the government of India under which that work will be multiplied by fifty times. In the small demonstration area, wheat production had been doubled by means that were simple and at hand. It is believed that this enlarged program, based on that demonstration, will, within five years, eliminate the threat of famine from India, and in ten years, will double India's present food production.

This work will be done under a special Indo-American Technical Cooperation Fund, to be jointly financed by the two governments. The fund will make possible the establishment of fifty rural-urban development areas, around river valley projects and tube wells. Each development area will have modern housing, good schools, improved health facilities, and many industrial opportunities. But that isn't all. The chain reaction of economic development, once started, goes far beyond the immediate range of Point Four work. The work of the fund is only one part of India's new five-year economic development plan. Under it, India, using the facilities of the Colombo Plan and of seven agencies of the United Nations, is making a concerted attack on illiteracy and disease, and will build roads, dams, power lines, factories, hospitals, and schools. Here is a program that illustrates the exciting possibilities that open up from the small beginnings of the Point Four project. . . .

Now, why is it we are carrying on this program? . . .

It is not philanthropy that motivates us. . . . There is a hard-headed self-interest in this program. . . .

We have an interest . . . in the development of representative and responsible governments in the world, since it creates an environment in which we can live peacefully and continue to develop our own society. This is the central purpose of our whole foreign policy.

But . . . we live in a time when two revolutionary movements have been criss-crossing the face of the earth. One of these is the revolution of technology, which in the nineteenth century brought industrialization to Western Europe and North America, and is now beginning to stir the countries called "underdeveloped."

The other revolution is represented by our Declaration of Independence and our Bill of Rights. . . .

It is the juncture of these revolutionary forces in the under-developed areas of the world that gives meaning to the Point Four Program. . . . If . . . we can help people not only to develop the soil, the water, and the resources of their lands, but to develop the culture that suits them and fits their needs, and to fulfill their aspirations for responsible and more representative government—then these revolutionary forces can be constructively channeled, and contribute to the peace of the world. If not, the world will continue to be swept by the rip tides of conflict.

Now if we look at the Point Four Program with these things in mind . . . we see that we cannot be indifferent to the social impact of our ideas and our science upon the people in these parts of the world. The revolutionary concepts I have mentioned, and Western education and science have had a powerful and disquieting impact upon some sections of the people in the so-called backward areas. . . .

The clash between modernism and traditionalism has been violent. The result has been bitter frustration, which has increased discontent and a search for radical solutions. . . .

This creates a complex problem for us in our relations with these areas. Our present security, in the face of the grave and immediate threat of aggression which hangs over the entire world, requires the maximum stability possible in these areas. But our long-term interests are best served if people's aspirations are fulfilled in a peaceful and orderly fashion. . . .

If, in our Point Four Program and all other activities that affect the underdeveloped areas, we seek to encourage and assist the governments of these countries to deal responsibly and effectively with the aspirations of the people, and by our influence and our aid assist in the development of representative institutions—then we shall be serving our own ultimate interests and the interests of world peace. . . .

Although I have not referred directly to the valuable technical assistance program carried on by the United Nations and its agencies, we consider our participation in that program an essential part of our Point Four activities. Support for the United Nations' program is central to the United States approach to technical assistance. We are proud to have played a leading part in the expansion of the United Nations Technical Assistance Program. Our experience has shown the wisdom of our intentions to continue to carry out these activities, wherever practicable, through the United Nations and its specialized agencies. This not only gives practical meaning to the Charter's reference to the United Nations as "a center for harmonizing the action of nations," but it makes full use of the United Nations' capacities for encouraging and assisting peaceful and orderly transitions.

NEW ROLE IN EUROPE [5]

When W. Averell Harriman took the oath of office . . . as Mutual Security Director . . . the American role in the Atlantic community was quietly but profoundly changed. The metamorphosis of the nation's foreign economic policy was now complete. Through clearly marked stages we had progressed from fairy godmother to stern governess, and finally to a fullfledged member of the family. As a contributor to the household budget we could now take sides in family arguments and rally the clan if unfriendly neighbors threatened.

[5] From "Harriman Has Triple Task in Europe," by Felix Belair, Jr., New York *Times* Washington correspondent. New York *Times*. p E6. November 4, 1951. Reprinted by permission.

The phased progress of the United States role in the economic relations of the Western world can be appreciated by a glance into the recent past. From schemes of postwar European relief, we went on to the Marshall Plan of European self-help. The threat of Communist aggression paved the way for the Mutual Defense Assistance program.

But not until economic and military aid were combined in the Mutual Security Program and both harnessed to the North Atlantic Treaty did the United States accept full partnership in the effort to solve Europe's economic problem. In embracing the task this government has made it a part of the economic problem of the free world.

Heretofore, the United States has taken part in the economic councils of Europe only as an "observer." Its participation has been limited to persuasion and to policing the use made of dollar aid. Europe might proposed, but as the power behind the purse strings it was for the United States to dispose. Now we assume the responsibilities of full partnership.

Where this challenging and uncharted course may lead our foreign economic policy it is probably too soon even to conjecture. But students of the subject think they do not overstate the possibilities when they say it could lead to the first effective marshaling of the resources of the free world or to a returning American isolationism not unlike that of the twenties. . . .

It is in the joint planning of expenditure of economic and military funds that the profundity of the change in this country's foreign economic relations is to be noted. Under the Marshall Plan the recipient governments got together each year through the Organization for European Economic Cooperation and prepared a "shopping list" of recovery needs to be supplied by the United States.

It was essentially a European shopping list and was so regarded by the ECA [Economic Cooperation Administration] which carefully screened it for nonessentials. It will not be a European shopping list that the Mutual Security Administration will send to Congress with a request for additional billions next February.

Through Mr. Harriman and his staff, the MSA will participate in its preparation. It will be as much American as European
in origin and will be presented as the shopping list of the free
world. Election years are hard on appropriations, especially when
the money is not to be spent on things that constituents can
see and appreciate.

In a very real sense, therefore, Congress will be called upon
each year to vote its confidence in or censure of the North Atlantic Treaty Organization, and it is in that process that some
students of the subject see the seeds of a possible retreat to
isolationism by the United States Congress.

Opponents of the Mutual Security Program will not be without weighty arguments. By the time Congress considers the
question, a substantial budgetary deficit will have become a
reality and the issue will recur whether the nation is justified in
carrying a substantial part of the free world's defense burden
along with its own.

Not until that issue is settled will the Western world know
whether it can continue looking to the United States for leadership.

COMMITMENTS UNDER NATO [6]

To meet the growing belligerence of the Russians and the
subversive activities of their stooges in the countries of western
and southern Europe, the Western nations took a number of defensive measures in the first half of 1947. These included the
following:

(1) On March 4 of that year Britain and France signed a
fifty-year mutual security agreement at Dunkirk.

(2) On March 12, alarmed by Communist strength and
British weakness in Greece, President Truman announced the
Truman Doctrine, which promised support to "free peoples who
are resisting attempted subjugation."

(3) On May 22 President Truman signed a $400 billion bill
passed by Congress to help bolster the economies and defenses of
Greece and Turkey.

[6] From "Growth of NATO: From a Senate Resolution to the Lisbon Conference," by James Reston, New York *Times* diplomatic correspondent. New York
Times. p E5. March 2, 1952. Reprinted by permission.

(4) On June 5 Secretary of State Marshall launched the historic program bearing his name.

Two provocative acts by the Communists early in 1948 demonstrated to the Western nations, however, that these decisions were not enough. In February of that year, the Communists staged their coup in Czechoslovakia, and in the spring they began the Berlin blockade.

This roughly was the sequence of events preceding the formation of the North Atlantic Treaty. The general idea about the North Atlantic Treaty . . . is that it was Senator Arthur H. Vandenberg's idea. . . . The procedure, however, was precisely the reverse. The sequence was from Robert A. Lovett, then Under Secretary of State and the present Secretary of Defense, to Mr. Vandenberg, who finally produced a draft Senate resolution stating that it was the "sense of the Senate" that the United States Government should, among other things, try to arrange the "association of the United States, by constitutional process, with such regional and other collective arrangements as are based on continuous and effective self-help and mutual aid, and as affect its national security."

This draft was completed May 11. It was adopted unanimously by the Foreign Relations Committee of the Senate May 19. Mr. Vandenberg called it up June 11, near the close of a busy session of Congress and just before the Presidential nominating convention of that year. It was adopted after very little debate, 64-6, and before many senators were aware of the historic nature of what was happening.

The treaty that developed from this beginning contained an article (Article 5) which reversed the whole trend of the traditional policy of the United States of "no entangling alliances." That article reads as follows:

> The parties agree that an armed attack against one or more of them in Europe or North America shall be considered an attack against them all; and consequently they agree that, if such an armed attack occurs, each of them . . . will assist the party or parties so attacked by taking forthwith, individually and in concert with the other parties, such action as it deems necessary, including the use of armed force, to restore and maintain the security of the North Atlantic area. . . .

The treaty containing this article was signed . . . April 4, 1949, by the representatives of the United States, Britain, France, Belgium, the Netherlands, Luxembourg, Portugal, Denmark, Norway, Italy, Iceland and Canada. It was ratified 82-13, by the United States Senate July 21, 1949, and part of the reason why the meaning of Article 5 has never really been understood in the country is that it was fogged up during the debate and overwhelmed by the secondary issue of whether a vote for the treaty obligated the United States to send arms to the treaty nations.

What was not understood then, however—though Secretary of State Dean Acheson explained it at the time—and what is not fully understood by some members of the Senate even today is that this Article 5 did contain a specific moral obligation, and a specific military obligation. The moral obligation was to treat an armed attack against one or more of the countries in the pact as an attack against the United States. And while the United States was left free to decide what action it deemed necessary in the event of an attack, it also took on a legal obligation to achieve a clear and specific objective, namely, "to restore and maintain the security of the North Atlantic area."

Neither the State Department nor the Senate foresaw at that time the development of the North Atlantic Treaty that has taken place since. They did not foresee the creation of a joint command in time of peace. They did not expect that United States troops would be sent to Europe to help form a peace-time barrier. They did not anticipate the long and bitter argument that has prevailed since over bringing a truncated Germany into the defense of Western Europe and into association with the North Atlantic Treaty.

What they had in mind was a simple idea that had become almost a political cliche in the last twenty-five years, namely, that if the Western powers—including the United States—had made clear in 1914 and 1939 that they would use all their resources against any nation that threatened areas vital to their security, there would have been no World War either time.

Two momentous events occurred soon thereafter, however, which changed the timetable and altered the whole formation of the Atlantic alliance. There were the atomic explosion in the Soviet Union and the Korean war.

The Soviet atomic explosion announced in September 1949 stepped up the formation of the military planning within the organization, and even led the treaty nations to accept the idea that they had to coordinate their rearmament program and pool their forces.

The Korean war, however, set in motion almost every development that has since preoccupied the North Atlantic Allies: the rearmament of the United States; the shipment of United States divisions to Europe; the creation of a North Atlantic commander in chief; the appointment of General Eisenhower to this post; the question of rearming the Germans; the movement toward European integration; the project to bring Greece and Turkey into the Atlantic alliance; the problem of rearming the West of Europe as fast as possible, and finally the delicate business of trying to reconcile this rearmament with the shaky economies and equally shaky nerves of a still badly shell-shocked continent.

While the United States was in the throes of rushing troops to Korea and planning the mobilization of the country, the French Government sent two memoranda to the United States, which explain as well as anything else the basic decisions that have led to all the activity within the Atlantic alliance in the last eighteen months.

The first of these arrived here August 5, 1950, and the second August 17, 1950. In these the French, alarmed by the Communist use of force in Korea and fearful that the Russians might really be planning the armed conquest of Western Europe, asked the United States a number of fundamental questions.

Did the United States think countries outside of Europe should contribute men to the defense of Western Europe and if so would the United States contribute forces of its own?

Did the United States think that such forces, if formed, should be integrated or merely operate as separate national units?

Did the United States believe such forces should be under a supreme commander?

And what did the United States think about the economics and financing of such an operation?

In explaining these questions, the French made it clear to the United States that France was not interested in an Allied strategy that depended primarily upon United States strategic airpower. By this they meant that they did not want to be "liberated" but to be "defended." In short, they wanted the United States to adopt a policy of defending Europe on the ground "as far east in Europe as possible."

Between August 17, 1950 and the middle of September, when the United States, British and French ministers met prior to the North Atlantic Council meeting in New York, the United States Government grappled with these basic questions and came out with a radically altered policy, which may very well be the subject of debate for many years.

The United States told France that it would accept the principle of sending more troops to Europe and of helping defend Western Europe "as far east as possible." It told France that it was for an integrated command under a single commander, but before the Joint Chiefs of Staff would approve these things, they insisted on one major condition: West Germany must be rearmed and brought into the defense of Western Europe. . . .

Not only were the other members of the Atlantic alliance asked to agree to the idea of bringing the Germans into the defense of the West, but they were asked to make major sacrifices for the rearmament and partial mobilization of an integrated force.

In short, the United States demanded what is now called a policy of being "operational in peacetime." That is to say, the United States rejected the old idea of waiting to form a unified command until the last hour of the emergency. The old policy of rearming at a leisurely pace was opposed. Instead, the idea of forming the command, raising the troops, gathering the allies, training the men and building the roads and airfields now—not later when a major war was imminent—was adopted.

SIGNIFICANCE OF THE EUROPEAN ARMY PLAN [7]

The signing of the West German peace contract and the
European Army agreement . . . combined to startle many people
here out of their personal preoccupations. The Administration
itself followed the two events with extraordinary interest, and
. . . even on the Hill many legislators were conscious of a great
event in the making.

Too many claims have been made on behalf of too many
events for too many years, however, for Washington to get very
enthusiastic, even over the possibility of Germany and France
standing together under the single command of a revolutionary
new European Army. . . .

Meanwhile, the European Army plan serves as a useful
pointer on the direction of United States policy in Europe,
especially since it was signed almost five years to the day after
the European Recovery Program was announced by former Secretary of State George C. Marshall at Harvard.

"Any assistance that this Government may render in the
future [to Europe]," General Marshall said in his Harvard
speech on June 5, 1947, "should provide a cure rather than a
mere palliative."

This is perhaps the basic difference between the policy-
makers of 1947 and the policy-makers of today. In 1947 some
of them still believed in cures, but now they're not so sure.

When General Marshall launched his program of economic
reconstruction, he was disillusioned in his efforts to negotiate
peace with the Russians, yet he was still able to hope that Western Europe could remain free and stable if only we would give
it substantial economic aid for a few years.

When Secretary of State Dean Acheson, the persistent match-
maker in this French-German affair, commented on the European
Army plan in Paris . . . however, his approach was somewhat
different.

[7] From "Now the U.S. Frontier Is Fixed at the Elbe," by James Reston,
New York *Times* diplomatic correspondent. New York *Times*. p E5. June 1,
1952. Reprinted by permission.

Mr. Acheson talked of the stability and security of Western Europe, not in terms of two or three years, as General Marshall had, but in terms of generations; not in terms of European co-operation alone, but in terms of trans-Atlantic cooperation; not in terms of "temporary aid," but in terms of the "enduring interests" of North America and Europe; not in terms of economic reconstruction, but in terms of military power.

Officials here no longer talk of quick cures but of "learning to live with our problems," and of sacrificing to do for a very long time to come.

What has led officials here to talk in this way is that they now see that every move in the cold war tends to lead to a counter-move and that this can go on for a very long time. . . .

In the five years between the European Recovery Program and the European Army program, various other changes have been made in United States and Western policy. Germany and Japan have been encouraged to try to refill the vacuum created by their defeat in World War II. The traditional United States policy of no entangling alliances has been abandoned. The movement toward economic and military integration in Western Europe has been pressed.

Coincidentally, the principle of opposing armed aggression with force has been defended; the strategy of helping defend Europe on the Elbe with American troops has replaced the old concept of liberating Western Europe after war breaks out. . . .

A strong coalition is growing in the West, despite many difficulties. It has demonstrated in Korea and elsewhere that no aggressor—no matter how powerful—can hope to seize areas vital to the security of the coalition without a major war.

This is an achievement that escaped French and British policy before 1914 and again before the outbreak of war in 1939; but it is an achievement that must be sustained from year to year without much hope of a "cure." That is the difference between the era of the European Recovery Program and the era of the European Army plan, which is just beginning.

SCHUMAN PLAN SUPPORT [8]

The Schuman plan . . . which owes its existence to the constant support of the United States, will continue to receive this support and in more concrete form than ever. The recently passed Mutual Security Act provides that the Schuman plan may receive financial aid from the funds to be voted for military and economic assistance to Europe. Thus there is Congressional authorization for the use of dollars to help the plan to get a start, and its success will be vitally affected by the financial resources at its disposal for loans to producers in the six countries.

Any producers or governments that might be tempted to sabotage the plan probably would hesitate to risk the loss not only of an indefinite amount of dollar aid but of the good will of the United States, which sees in the plan a vital step toward the integration of Europe. Therefore it may be said that a kind of United States guarantee stands behind this project, as well as behind the treaty for a European Defense Community—twin designs for the tight linking-up of the Bonn Republic with France and her neighbors and with the North Atlantic defense system.

EXAMPLES OF INTERNATIONAL AGREEMENTS [9]

Among the many agreements [1274 as of December 31, 1950] . . . are such multilaterals as the General Agreement on Tariffs and Trade, the Convention on International Civil Aviation, the Articles of Agreement of the International Bank for Reconstruction and Development and of the International Monetary Fund, the International Sanitary Convention for Aerial Navigation, the Charter of the United Nations and Statute of the International Court of Justice, the agreements establishing the constitutions of FAO, UNESCO, WHO, and ILO, the International Convention for the Regulation of Whaling, the Inter-

[8] From "Now the Schuman Plan Is Nearer to Reality," by Harold Callender, chief of New York *Times* Paris bureau. New York *Times*. p E3. June 22, 1952. Reprinted by permission.

[9] From "Part II, Sixth Release, United States Treaty Developments," press release, May 19, 1952, *United States Department of State Bulletin.* 26:967. June 16, 1952.

American Treaty of Reciprocal Assistance, the International Tele-communication Convention and Radio Regulations (Atlantic City, 1947), the convention for the unification of certain rules relating to international transportation by air, the convention for limiting the manufacture of narcotic drugs, the agreement re-garding the regulation of production and marketing of sugar, the International Wheat Agreement, the North Atlantic Treaty, and others, as well as numerous important bilateral agreements between the United States and fifty other countries relating to a wide range of subjects.

EXECUTIVE AGREEMENTS IN FORCE [10]

One hundred eleven (111) agreements governing technical aspects of commercial aviation have been made within the frame-work of the International Civil Aviation Convention . . .; 105 economic and technical agreements, including Point Four agree-ments, have been made under the Economic Cooperation Act of 1948 and the Foreign Aid Appropriation Act of 1949; and 25 mutual defense assistance agreements have been made under the Mutual Defense Assistance Act of 1949 and the Mutual Security Act of 1951. The "Institute of Inter-American Affairs Act" has been the statutory basis for over a hundred agreements setting up cooperative programs in the fields of health and sani-tation, agriculture, development of productive resources, and education. Other examples are agreements in the fields of ship-ping, radio communications, taxation, the work of American military and technical missions abroad; and there are many others.

AMERICAN PARTICIPATION IN INTERNATIONAL CONFERENCES [11]

In considering the extent of American participation in inter-national organizations, past, present and future, it should be

[10] From "Senate Resolutions Proposing Restrictions on Treaty-Making Powers," statement by Acting Secretary of State David K. E. Bruce. *United States Depart-ment of State Bulletin.* 26:960-1. June 16, 1952.

[11] Based upon calendar of meetings of international organizations and confer-ences prepared by the Division of International Conferences, Department of State, April 25, 1952. *United States Department of State Bulletin.* 26:710-12. May 5, 1952.

noted that the number of international conferences going on at this very moment seems almost unbelievable to anyone viewing international relations in terms of American participation in the 1920's.

More than a hundred different international meetings of one sort or another were in progress during the three-month period, April to July, 1952. Few of these were solely political in extent. Most were dealing with economic and social matters on a regional or global scale.

They included such diverse sessions as these:

International Civil Aviation Organization.....Montreal
Tripartite Conference on Aid to Yugoslavia..Washington
UN Trusteeship Council..................New York
UN International Children's Emergency Fund—World Health Organization Joint Committee on Health Policy ....New York
UN Economic and Social Council: Commission on Status of Women............................Geneva
UNESCO: International Symposium on Arid Zone Hydrology ....Ankara
4th Inter-American Conference on Social Security......
.... Mexico City
International Telecommunication Union.....The Hague
NATO: Petroleum Planning Committee....Washington
International Labor Organization: 5th Regional Conference of American States Members....Rio de Janeiro
Pan-American Sanitary Organization......Washington
International Wheat Council.................London
South Pacific Commission...................Noumea
Diplomatic Conference on Maritime Law......Brussels
Universal Postal Union: 13th Congress........Brussels
Caribbean Commission .... Guadeloupe
Food and Agriculture Organization: International Rice Commission ....Bandung, Indonesia
International Rubber Study Group.............Ottawa
International Symposium on Problems of Desert Research ....Jerusalem

6th International Hydrographic Conference..... Monaco
International Cotton Advisory Committee........ Rome
World Meteorological Organization: Regional Associa-
    tion for Europe......................... Zurich
International Conference on Large Electric High Tension
    Systems .... Paris
International Convention for Protection of Industrial
    Property .... Vienna
International Whaling Commission........... London
International Criminal Policy Commission.... Stockholm

THE UNITED NATIONS: SUCCESS OR FAILURE?

EDITOR'S INTRODUCTION

Time and again it has been repeated that the United Nations is the cornerstone of American foreign policy. But the meaning of this statement has not been too clear and many people both here and abroad are still confused as to the relationship between American foreign policy and the United Nations.

Part of the problem unquestionably is due to lack of adequate information about the details of United States—United Nations cooperation. Of course, the President makes an annual report to the Congress in which he reviews the extent of American participation in the UN. But most of the confusion seems to stem from lack of information about the UN itself, its purposes and its limitations. The rising tide of criticism of the UN in the United States can be traced directly to the Korean conflict and the lack of support of American policy by many UN members. As a result, expressed impatience and a search for other solutions have become widespread.

Even before the Korean affair, however, attempts were being made to "strengthen the UN." The original approach was in the direction of revision of the UN charter to offset the Soviet veto. After the outbreak of fighting in Korea the proposals for strengthening the UN began more and more frequently to take the form of suggestions for a super-government, a world federation. Congress gave the matter serious consideration in committee hearings in 1949 and 1950, but was unable to find a specific solution supported by enough public opinion to justify any radical shift in foreign policy. The State Department attitude was to "keep what we have and make it work" rather than look for new and untried solutions.

But the reaction of the American public has not been quite as favorable to the UN. In June 1952 a former high-ranking

member of the United States delegation to the UN, Porter Mc-
Keever, conceded that public support of the UN "was slipping."
He believed that loss of confidence in the international organiza-
tion was due to the American government's failure to use the
UN more effectively in behalf of our own foreign policy.

An increasing volume of criticism has been heard in recent
months, stemming in part from the deadlock in peace negotiations in Korea, in part from growing alarm on the part of taxpayers as they watch taxes mount to finance national security
and foreign assistance programs. Even though Congress and the
public at large seem to be unwilling to abandon the UN completely, fears of an overburdened economy led the Republicans
to include a foreign policy plank in their 1952 campaign platform of limiting economic and military aid abroad "to what we
can afford."

All this adds up to the question: How much longer will the
American public foot the bill for free world defense? So it
becomes increasingly important to evaluate American participation
in the United Nations, its over-all success and failure in terms
of our own national interest, to see what hope the future holds
for the success of American foreign policy through the UN.

UN AS BASIS OF AMERICAN FOREIGN POLICY [1]

The broad objectives of the United Nations and of United
States foreign policy are very similar. Then Deputy Under Secretary of State Rusk testified that a "well-considered and con-
venient statement of our (United States) basic policy is found
in the preamble and articles 1 and 2 of the Charter of the United
Nations." This position is supported by practice as can be seen
by reference to cases, such as Greece, Korea, and Iran before
the United Nations, which received the full support of the
United States.

More specifically, the United States opposes aggression anywhere at any time. The United Nations Charter provides the

[1] From "Revision of the United Nations Charter," report of the Senate Committee on Foreign Relations, September 1, 1950. (Senate Report no2501) 81st
Congress, 2d session. Superintendent of Documents. Washington, D.C. 1950.
p 18-20, 22-4.

necessary machinery and the basic obligations and commitments necessary for the cooperation of all states opposed to aggression. In this sense the United States and the UN move in the same direction. The existence of the UN therefore facilitates the achievement of our purposes.

The United Nations, in fact, affords a means whereby collective self-defense agreements may be developed without their becoming so exclusive as to disrupt the growing community of nations.

United Nations membership makes it a duty for the United States, as a leading United Nations member, and for every other member, to concern themselves with important world problems wherever they may arise. To the degree to which United States support of the United Nations is genuine and sincere it is possible to transform the East-West struggle into a USSR-United Nations struggle in a manner permitting suitable recognition of the interests of the world community as a whole.

The President recently stated the position of the United States with respect to the United Nations, as follows:

> We support the United Nations and keep this contract because the Charter expresses our fundamental aims in the modern world. We know that the fulfillment of the Charter will best advance our own vital interests—to attain peace with justice, to assure freedom, and to bring about economic and social progress, for ourselves and all peoples. It is for this reason that support of the United Nations is and must be point 1 of our foreign policy. . . .

The United States Government in its efforts to strengthen the United Nations has not suggested amendment of the Charter. Instead, its efforts have been directed toward making the Charter work. Mr. Dean Rusk, then Deputy Under Secretary of State, said that "the Charter is our basic over-all agreement with the Soviet Union." It contains, he added, "provisions which, if loyally carried out, would insure the peace." "We do not need another over-all agreement; we need performance on the ones we already have."

The practice of the United States in the United Nations is evidence of this Government's sincerity in trying to make the Charter work. President Truman in his inaugural address said:

"We will continue to search for way to strengthen their [the United Nations and related agencies] authority and increase their effectiveness." The United States has endeavored to give a liberal interpretation to the provisions of the Charter. It has done its best to adhere to the terms as well as the spirit of the Charter and, in cases like those of Greece and Korea, the United States has, consistent with the action of the United Nations, given direct aid to those countries. The United States has sought voluntary agreement to curb the use of the veto; it has encouraged the development of the General Assembly as an instrument of peace; it has refrained from the use of the veto; it has loaned material and men to the United Nations to assist it in carrying out its functions. The United States has spared no effort in trying to get the Charter to work.

Mr. Rusk commented on the great diversity of this Government's efforts to strengthen international organizations, including the United Nations, as follows:

The great diversity of our effort is well illustrated by a brief reference to the legislative problems in the field of foreign affairs now before the Congress. The effort to strengthen the United Nations and its related agencies is represented by the Charter of the International Trade Organization, by the Point Four Program, by Palestine refugee legislation, by proposals to lift certain ceilings on United States contributions to international organizations, by the Convention on Privileges and Immunities of the United Nations, by the proposed Genocide Convention, and others. Current legislative measures designed to strengthen the free world include renewal of the mutual defense assistance program, continuation of the Economic Cooperation Act, the Charter of the Organization of the American States, and legislation to provide privileges and immunities for members of the Council of the Organization of American States.

While some of these proposals are unimportant when compared to the giant issues that confront world organization, all are illustrative of the attempts being made to move in the direction of giving international organizations the instruments and the backing they need if they are to work.

The Congress has encouraged the executive in its efforts to strengthen the United Nations. It has gone further. It has encouraged the organization of the free world to fight economic chaos and the threat of aggression. . . .

The fate of the League of Nations was determined by incidents in such far-away places as Manchuria and Ethiopia. The United Nations now faces its greatest test in far-away Korea. But there the similarity ends. Instead of hesitation and uncertainty the United Nations has acted firmly and boldly to meet the threat to the peace that was posed by the attack of North Korea on the United Nations-sponsored government of the Republic of Korea. . . .

The question will undoubtedly be raised as to whether the United States is "using" the United Nations in Korea or whether the United Nations is "using" the United States. The action which has been taken there is a United Nations action. It is supported by fifty-one United Nations members, the United States among them. These nations have a common interest in defending the policy set forth in Article 1 of the Charter, which reads in part:

The purposes of the United Nations are: 1. To maintain international peace and security, and to that end: to take effective collective measures for the prevention and removal of threats to the peace, and for the suppression of acts of aggression. . . .

It is difficult to tell what the effect of the Korean situation may be on the United Nations. . . . Soviet reaction to United Nations firmness in Korea might be directed toward attempting to destroy the United Nations . . . and the idea of collective security by withdrawing from the United Nations.

Fortunately, even though the Soviet could endeavor to destroy the United Nations either from within or without, the United States can, with the help of the free world, preserve the United Nations and make it into an effective force on the side of freedom and law. . . . The North Atlantic Pact and the Rio Treaty clearly show that nations have a right to organize under the self-defense provisions of Article 51 or the regional arrangement provisions of the Charter in order to defend themselves against attack. Perhaps the time has come to explore the possibility of concluding similar pacts for the Near East and the Far East so the countries of those areas can benefit by collective self-defense arrangements.

There is still another avenue open in the event the Soviet Union endeavors to use the veto to destroy the United Nations. Since the Security Council is the only United Nations agency where the veto applies, that agency can be relegated to a secondary position, and more and more of the difficult problems turned over to the General Assembly for solution. The Assembly has authority under the Charter to make recommendations relating to world peace and its decisions are taken by a two-thirds majority vote.

If the Soviets try to kill the United Nations by formally withdrawing from the organization, constructive leadership on the part of the free nations could lead to the creation of a new or revitalized organization of the free nations of the world. Article 109 of the Charter makes provision for the calling of a general conference of members by a two-thirds vote of the General Assembly and a vote of any seven members of the Security Council. Thus if the Soviet Union should withdraw from the United Nations, the Charter provides a vetoless way for calling a Conference which might deal with such a situation. . . . The present Charter has within it certain resources for strengthening collective security regardless of the attitude of any one of the Big Five. The Charter has within it the means for reorganizing the United Nations if Soviet action leads to demands for such reorganization. The Charter will carry far more traffic if the nations want it to do so. The Korean action shows that. The position of the freedom-loving nations of the world is tremendously strengthened by the existence of the United Nations. As the United Nations is strengthened so will be our freedoms.

ECONOMIC AND SOCIAL ACCOMPLISHMENTS OF THE UN [2]

The United Nations, together with the specialized agencies, provide a framework for international collaboration in important spheres of activity in the economic and social field.

[2] From "Revision of the United Nations Charter," report of the Senate Committee on Foreign Relations, September 1, 1950. (Senate Report no2501) 81st Congress, 2d session. Superintendent of Documents. Washington, D.C. 1950. p 13-15.

None of the specialized agencies exercise any direct legislative powers. However, the programs which they have developed illustrate the widespread interest of governments in utilizing this machinery for promoting conditions of stability and well-being which are necessary for peaceful relations among nations. Moreover, this machinery is sufficiently flexible to enable member countries to work on problems of real concern to them, uninhibited by the veto or by the reluctance of the Soviet Union to participate in programs looking toward specific objectives. A brief review of some of the accomplishments in the economic and social field will serve not only to indicate the accelerated pace of international collaboration, but also to illustrate the wide scope of the problems being dealt with.

The Food and Agriculture Organization is engaged in the development of programs looking toward the better utilization of world-wide agricultural resources to meet the food requirements of expanding populations. Its chief efforts have been concerned with methods of improving production of agricultural products and dealing with major threats to food supplies. It has taken steps, for example, looking toward increasing production and improving the utilization of rice, the principal item of diet for many peoples, particularly in the Far East, and toward the stimulation of increased fish production by development of new fish resources.

In the financial field, the International Bank and the International Monetary Fund have significant roles to play. The bank, with a subscribed capital of $8,323,500,000, of which $1,664,-000,000 has been called, has made loans totaling over $832,845,-000 for productive enterprises in fifteen different countries. In addition, it has rendered valuable services to a number of governments in the form of surveys and advice in connection with their national development programs. The International Monetary Fund has not only assisted countries in the stabilization of their currencies but has also provided technical advice to governments on their currency, banking, and allied problems.

In the field of communications, the Universal Postal Union and the International Telecommunications Union are engaged in the adoption of regulations to meet modern requirements.

The expansion of air traffic over land and sea throughout the world has required extensive international cooperation in the development of safety regulations and aids to navigation to insure safe flight. The International Civil Aviation Organization has developed numerous regulations which have promoted safety in international air travel.

Two major refugee problems have been tackled by the United Nations. Nearly 1,000,000 European refugees and displaced persons had to be taken care of when the International Refugee Organization began operations in July 1947, after the termination of UNRRA [United Nations Relief and Rehabilitation Administration]. At the end of October 1949, the IRO had reestablished over 700,000 and was still providing care and maintenance for approximately 345,000 in camps. When the IRO is terminated, the major task of reestablishing most of these refugees will have been completed. This is the first time in history that governments have shown their willingness to contribute funds on a large enough scale to solve a major refugee problem through an international organization. Over three-quarters of a million refugees who were victims of the hostilities between Israel and the Arab States, likewise have been cared for by the United Nations Relief for Palestine Refugees, an agency set up by the General Assembly of the United Nations. Its successor agency, the United Nations Relief and Works Agency for Palestine Refugees, is designed to provide employment for the refugees on useful projects in lieu of direct relief.

Through the International Children's Emergency Fund, large-scale efforts have been undertaken to aid war victims who could not readily be aided by other means. This emergency program has reflected the interest of governments in aiding undernourished children and improving their health at a cost of nearly $150,000,000.

The World Health Organization has undertaken to attack disease at its source without regard to national boundaries instead of working on a nation-by-nation basis as did the International Office of Public Health before the war. Among other things, it is undertaking important programs for the control of man's worst diseases—particularly malaria, tuberculosis, and venereal disease—in strategically located areas of the world.

The International Labor Organization, established at the end of the first World War, has adopted a large number of international conventions and recommendations for the improvement of conditions of workers. As a specialized agency of the United Nations, it is now dealing with the difficult problems of manpower and migration and tackling other current problems affecting conditions of employment.

The economic and social aspects of the Charter probably could, if given enough scope and enough support, accomplish dramatic results in stimulating the development of the world's underdeveloped areas and in so increasing the welfare of the inhabitants as to reduce significantly the likelihood of their succumbing to Communist penetration. . . .

UN SIXTH ANNUAL REPORT—EXCERPTS [3]

The United Nations . . . was founded on the assumption that the five great powers which led the struggle against Nazi Germany, Fascist Italy and imperialist Japan would continue to cooperate in the peace that followed victory. Since the events of the past six years have led to a different result, some have come to the conclusion that the United Nations in its present form is not a workable instrument for peace and security, at least in the foreseeable future. A few would scrap the organization altogether. A greater number would seek peace and security mainly by other means, while conserving the United Nations in a secondary position as a forum for world debate and a useful vehicle for international cooperation in economic and social matters. . . .

It is important to recall that the founding of the United Nations was motivated by a far more fundamental and lasting concept . . . than a passing wartime alliance of great powers. This is that the peace and well-being of all nations and peoples

[3] From "A Report on the United Nations," excerpts from the sixth annual report to the General Assembly by Secretary General Trygve Lie. *Current History.* 22:39-46. January 1952. Reprinted by permission.

have become in the present age so intimately interrelated that it is necessary for them, despite all their differences, to join in a world-wide organization looking toward security from war, freedom and independence for the peoples, and mutual economic and social progress. . . .

But the founders of our organization never conceived that its mere establishment would of itself remove or prevent conflicts and differences of national interests, aspirations, cultures and beliefs, nor would it assure in advance the future good conduct and good faith of governments in all circumstances. On the contrary, they considered that from that time forward a world organization was the one essential and primary instrument, to be available in all circumstances, through which the member nations could over a period of time develop adequate means for controlling unlawful international conduct on the part of any government and for preventing those differences which inevitably arise between nations from leading to further world wars, with the consequent denial or destruction of the political, economic and social progress of the peoples. . . . When we consider the role of the United Nations in relation to attempts to settle peacefully disputes between nations and to prevent or put an end to armed conflicts, we find that virtually all the most serious questions of the past six years with the exception of the conclusion of the actual peace treaties, have been brought in one form or another to the United Nations.

In all . . . activities of the United Nations in the political sphere, definite decisions have been taken or recommendations made. . . . The governments of members have found it both wise and necessary to resort to the United Nations in their effort to settle, ameliorate, or at least contain, most of the dangerous differences and disputes that have arisen among them since the end of the second World War, including those directly involving the interests of the great powers.

The general practice has been to bring serious disputes even of a primarily regional character to the world organization for a hearing, for the judgment of world opinion as reflected in its organs, and for the deployment of its resources in negotiation, mediation and conciliation, and in the recommendation of settlements. This practice, in turn, seems to support the basic judgment embodied in the Charter that, in a world so closely interrelated as ours today, a serious dispute between nations in one part of the world is the concern of nations in all parts of the world. . . .

In spite of the lack of unanimity of the permanent members of the Security Council, United Nations action has resulted in bringing about the peaceful settlement of a substantial number of serious international issues in the first six years of its existence. In other cases not yet settled, United Nations action has prevented or halted armed conflict. In still others, where little or no success has yet been achieved, governments have nevertheless found no feasible alternative, no way offering a better prospect of ultimate success, than that of continuing their efforts in and through the organization. . . .

Armed aggression anywhere, or the threat of armed conflict anywhere, is, in fact as well as in theory, becoming more and more the concern of nations everywhere. The most striking demonstration of this has been in Korea. There, for the first time in history, armed collective security action against military aggression by a world organization has been undertaken, not under some regional pact or traditional alliance, but by and under the United Nations. . . .

Finally, there are the "Uniting for Peace" resolutions, adopted by the General Assembly at its last session, which aim at the development of an effective collective security system which could immediately be set in motion in case of an emergency.

These resolutions, I hope, reflect the beginning of a significant evolution in the policies of the governments of most member states concerning the whole problem of security from aggression. . . . Has the universal approach represented by the United Nations Charter and system proved in practice to be wise and necessary, above and beyond the likewise important national and regional efforts toward these ends?

It is true that by far the largest international programs of economic aid for recovery from the effect of the second World War have been carried on outside the United Nations, although they have contributed greatly to the capacity of the participating nations to join in achieving the objectives of the Charter. Outside these programs, however, the United Nations system on the whole is gradually developing into the main center for international planning and action of both an emergency and a longer-term character toward these goals.

To demonstrate the scope of the organization's activity it is only necessary to recall the work carried on under the Economic and Social Council, with its three regional economic commissions and its nine "functional" commissions dealing with world-wide economic and social problems, as well as the work of the eleven specialized agencies—the International Labor Organization with 64 members, the Food and Agriculture Organization with 66, the United Nations Educational, Scientific and Cultural Organization with 64, the International Civil Aviation Organization with 57, the World Health Organization with 78, the International Bank for Reconstruction and Development and the International Monetary Fund, each with 50, the Universal Postal Union with 86, the International Refugee Organization with 18, and the World Meteorological Organization with 66. It is hoped that the Intergovernmental Maritime Consultative Organization will be brought into operation in the near future and, in addition, the General Agreements on Tariffs and Trade are now provisionally in force among thirty-two nations.

Under the United Nations itself, and directly responsible to the General Assembly, are the Relief and Works Agency for Palestine refugees, the Korean Reconstruction Agency, the International Children's Emergency Fund, and the newly established Office of the High Commissioner for Refugees.

I come now to a nonpolitical activity that is of prime importance to the achievement of long-term stability in many parts of the world. I refer, of course, to the technical assistance program for economic development, social welfare and public administration. . . .

The main fields of technical assistance activity of the United Nations and the specialized agencies are economic development, agriculture and health programs, wide educational and vocational training schemes, social welfare in its limitless variety and, finally, the improvement of public administration, without which effective social organization and action are not possible in the modern state.

Both the regular and expanded program of the United Nations and the specialized agencies have made substantial and heartening progress in the past year. Reviewing the work of the United Nations and the agencies together, over 500 requests have been received from sixty-four countries, and agreements have been signed with forty-five governments to provide experts and other assistance carried on by the United Nations and the specialized agencies in their respective fields of action. It should be said that these programs are being developed side by side with bilateral and regional programs of technical assistance outside the United Nations system.

In the field of social welfare and human rights, there has been an increasing recognition of the solemn obligations imposed by the Charter. The Universal Declaration of Human Rights stands as a beacon of hope and progress for peoples everywhere. Its potentially vast effect upon the future of mankind has as yet only begun to make itself manifest, but the trend is already apparent. Parts of the Declaration are being written into national constitutions, while civil rights in other countries are upheld by references to it. . . .

During the past six years, the United Nations has clearly become the main international instrument for the advancement of dependent peoples toward self-government and independence. In addition to the trusteeship system, which now covers eleven trust territories, the principle of international accountability and concern for all dependent territories is being applied.

Virtually all important developments in the evolution of international law during the past six years have been closely connected with the United Nations. The Charter itself has become the central instrument of international law, and one of the most important features of the development of that law is the continuing and cumulative effort to implement the Charter in all its aspects. Apart from the Charter, various international conventions designed to develop or clarify international law have been or are being prepared under United Nations auspices. The Convention on the Prevention and Punishment of the Crime of

Genocide was adopted by the General Assembly and is now in force, although a number of important member states have not yet ratified it. A convention on the status of refugees has been completed this year. The establishment of a court to judge crimes under international law is being studied. The International Law Commission has produced a number of valuable drafts, including a draft code of offenses against the peace and security of mankind. There has been an increasing tendency for states to refer their legal disputes to the International Court of Justice, which has declared the existing state of the law in six judgments and seven advisory opinions.

What conclusions should be drawn from a review even so necessarily brief and incomplete as the above?

The first is that, in these matters as in political questions, the governments of member states have once again confirmed in practice the concept reflected in the United Nations Charter that world organization is essential for the advancement of the welfare of their peoples.

A second conclusion to be drawn from the record is that already many important programs benefiting hundreds of millions of people throughout the world have been promoted through the United Nations system with good results. There have been and continue to be setbacks, failures, disappointments. The great political conflicts of our time inevitably have reduced the effectiveness of some, though not all, of these programs.

At best, the rate of progress is slow in projects involving the voluntary cooperation of many nations. Viewed from year to year, the lag between proposal and debate on the one hand, and performance on the other, has often seemed disheartening. But over a period of six years, the perspective, I claim, is different.

It seems to me that the record of the past six years has shown the United Nations to be a practical instrument for all nations seeking peace, security and the well-being and advancement of their peoples.

The organization is still in its early stages of development. No matter how right its principles or how practical its machinery have proved to be in many fields, the United Nations depends for its ultimate success upon the extent of the support given to these principles and the use made of this machinery by member states. Unless these are realized in sufficient measure, there is danger that the bitter conflicts and historic upheavals of our times may prove too great a strain for a world structure that is still in the early stages of development.

I believe this disaster may be avoided if the governments will act promptly, vigorously and wisely to make the United Nations —in fact and in all respects—a cornerstone of their foreign policy, and thus further strengthen the power of the United Nations to maintain peace, to develop more friendly relations, and to work toward a better and fairer distribution of the resources of the earth. . . . I think it important that the governments of members should express more clearly and explicitly the commitment—subject of course to their respective constitutional processes and to the obligations of self-defense—of their foreign policy, their armed forces and their economic power to this developing world-wide system of collective security.

There should be no conflict between obligations arising, on the one hand, from regional and mutual defense pacts concluded in conformity with the Charter and obligations arising, on the other hand, from the United Nations collective security system. Any serious threat or act of armed aggression calling for action under such pacts will also call for action by the United Nations itself, since the latter must, under the Charter, always be concerned whenever and wherever peace is threatened or broken. Furthermore, it is not possible to achieve lasting security from war by regional pacts alone. At best, those pacts can of themselves only lead to a precarious balance of power.

It is, I believe, in the vital national interest of member states desiring peace that their regional security commitments be more clearly regarded as complementary to their primary obligation to join in defending world peace under the United Nations. This is essential if the United Nations is to develop a world collective security system that will be a really effective deterrent to armed aggression and a barrier against war. . . .

The reasons which prompted the framers of the Charter to place the primary responsibility for peace and security upon the Security Council are as sound today as they were in 1945. There can be no lasting peace in the world unless a peaceful settlement can be achieved between the two groups of great powers, and a peaceful settlement is something that, in the end, can be reached only by negotiations, mutual concession and the development of mutual confidence.

I believe that the development of a strong and effective United Nations collective security system, combined with renewed efforts at mediation and conciliation, can improve the chances of ameliorating and, in time, settling the great political conflicts that most endanger world peace today. The greater the ability of the United Nations to foil attempts to solve conflicts of national interest by force, the more likely will it be that those conflicts can be settled by negotiation. A realization of the political stresses of the day is essential to the achievement of lasting settlements. . . .

It is my deep conviction that it would be a grave mistake to permit the pressures, great as they are, of immediate political and military problems to distract the United Nations from those longer-range problems upon the settlement of which international stability and good feeling will greatly depend, namely, those concerned with raising the living standards of peoples everywhere, particularly of those nations which have yet to attain a reasonable level of subsistence for the great mass of their populations.

The United Nations must never forget that its functions are not "peace-keeping" but "peace-creating," and that the creation of conditions of peace will in a large measure be the result of providing the economic and psychological framework within which the majority of mankind finds life livable and worth while.

THE ACHESON PLAN [4]

Since the Acheson plan constitutes the principal step taken during the past year to strengthen the United Nations, it may be well to recall its provisions. . . .

[4] From "The Acheson Plan for the UN." by Carl Marcy, staff associate, and Francis O. Wilcox, chief of staff of the Senate Committee on Foreign Relations. *Foreign Policy Reports.* 27:60-1. May 15, 1951. Reprinted by permission.

The main objective of the Uniting for Peace resolution was to organize the General Assembly so that in the future it could take effective action in the maintenance of peace should the Security Council find itself hamstrung by the veto. The resolution was based on the hard lessons learned from the Korean experience.

The Acheson plan was adopted by the General Assembly on November 3, 1950 by a 52-5 vote with only two abstentions. The principal provisions of the resolution are as follows:

1. If the Security Council fails to exercise its primary responsibility for the maintenance of peace because of the lack of unanimity of the permanent members, the General Assembly "shall consider the matter immediately" and may meet within twenty-four hours (instead of two weeks) after a request for such a meeting is received.

2. The General Assembly may make "appropriate recommendations to members for collective measures, including, in the case of a breach of the peace or act of aggression, the use of armed force when necessary."

3. The resolution establishes a "Peace Observation Commission" with fourteen members, including the United States and the USSR. This commission "could observe and report on the situation in any area where there exists international tension the continuance of which is likely to endanger the maintenance of international peace and security."

4. The resolution recommends that each member of the United Nations "maintain within its national armed forces elements so trained, organized and equipped that they could promptly be made available, in accordance with its constitutional processes, for service as a United Nations unit or units, upon recommendation by the Security Council or General Assembly."

5. Finally, the resolution establishes a Collective Measures Committee of fourteen members, including France, the United Kingdom and the United States but not including the USSR. This commission was directed "to study and make a report to the Security Council and the General Assembly, not later than September 1, 1951 on methods . . . which might be used to

maintain and strengthen international peace and security. . . .

The UN has once again formally subscribed to the proposition that aggression will be opposed by the armed strength of the international community, if necessary. It seems likely, however, that the amount of force given in support of this proposition will be in direct ratio to the involvement of the security interests of a given state. . . .

This resolution in some respects incorporates on a worldwide basis certain principles of the Atlantic pact. While the Atlantic pact emphasizes that an attack on one is an attack on all and commits the parties to take whatever action is necessary to restore and maintain the security of the North Atlantic area, the Uniting for Peace resolution declares that an act of aggression calls for the United Nations to recommend the use of collective measures against the aggressor. In the case of both the Atlantic pact and the peace resolution, the nature and extent of the measures which each state will take depend on its own constitutional processes and its own judgment of what it can and should do under the circumstances. . . .

In the final analysis, the resolution, while strengthening the United Nations procedurally, still depends for its effectiveness on the will and power of the members. The will of the members, in turn, depends on their evaluation of the immediate threat of a particular aggression to their own security. As aggression traceable to the same source recurs, members may gradually realize that aggression against one is a subtle but calculated aggression against all. As that realization becomes more widespread, there is a possibility that the Uniting for Peace resolution may become a powerful force in welding the free world into a working instrument to prevent war. . . .

Progress made under the Acheson plan . . . is real progress in the right direction. Under the circumstances, however, the sponsors of the various congressional resolutions would probably not be willing to accept the Acheson plan as a satisfactory substitute for their own more far-reaching proposals.

RESULTS OF THE 1951 SESSION [5]

Despite the expressions of optimism from those in official positions, most delegates at the 1951 session of the United Nations General Assembly had decided by the time it adjourned that it was one of the least constructive in the history of the world organization. Except for the routine work of approving the United Nations budget and filling vacancies in United Nations organs, the positive accomplishments resulting from the three months of debate were confined to two:

(1) The United Nations Disarmament Commission was created and instructed to proceed in accordance with the views of the United States and other Western powers on methods of bringing about disarmament and the eventual prohibition of atomic weapons.

(2) The Assembly asked the Collective Measures Committee to continue its work for another year, although it failed to approve the recommendations drawn up by the committee regarding the utilization of armed forces against an aggressor.

Both actions were vigorously opposed by the Soviet Union, and in fact the Assembly once more refused to approve a single important Soviet proposal. The parting statements by Andrei A. Vishinsky, Soviet Foreign Minister, and Jacob A. Malik, chief Soviet delegate, were most pessimistic.

Also according to precedent, not a single important resolution supported by the United States failed to carry. But the United States encountered much stronger opposition to some of its proposals than in the past, even though this opposition often was expressed by abstentions rather than by out-and-out votes against.

Since real accomplishments were in short supply, any judgment on the work of the 1951 session must be based mainly on the question whether the United States or the Soviet Union emerged in a stronger propaganda position than when the Assembly convened last November.

[5] From "UN Propaganda Battle Is Regarded as a Draw," by Thomas J. Hamilton, chief of New York *Times* UN Bureau. New York *Times*. p E9. February 10, 1952. Reprinted by permission.

The preparation of a box score on the current session is complicated by these two factors:

(1) The mere fact that a United States resolution gets a majority in the Assembly, or even an overwhelming majority, does not mean that the Soviet Union has lost. The United States managed, although with great difficulty, to elect Greece to the Security Council over Byelorussia, but it seems clear that, whatever advantages may accrue later, a substantial number of people in non-Communist countries disapproved and in fact considered it another example of United States intransigence.

(2) Although Mr. Vishinsky remained on hand to give a push when he could, the troubles encountered by the United States arose mainly from a revolt by the Arab and Asian countries, especially the Arabs, against Western leadership. The United States bore the brunt of it because, while it has gone along in the past with the steadily increasing movement in the Assembly in favor of independence for virtually everybody, this time it sided with its North Atlantic allies—who also, as the Soviet delegates like to note, are colonial powers.

Mr. Vishinsky, who was off his game anyway, offered little difficulty with purely Soviet proposals. The only Soviet maneuver that contained the possibilities of trouble for the United States was his proposal for a special high-level meeting of the Security Council to "facilitate" an armistice in Korea, but this was badly handled and was finally dismissed without much difficulty.

The violence of Mr. Vishinsky's attack on the United States in this connection, and his insistence on debating the same issues that were being discussed at Panmunjom, made it very easy for the United States to persuade the delegates that it would be unwise for the Assembly to take up a permanent settlement of the Korean question until there was an armistice.

The fact that only the Soviet bloc voted against postponing the question until an armistice had been reached or there were "other developments," was encouraging to the United States. Still more encouraging was the fact that there were only two abstentions, and that India and Indonesia, which had become habitual abstainers at this session, voted with the United States against the Soviet Union.

Still, the rejection of the postponement resolution would have been a slap in the face for the United States, and it is hard to share the enthusiasm of Ernest A. Gross, who said a vote for it constituted a vote of confidence for the conduct of the Allies on the armistice negotiations.

The principal entry on the credit side of the United States ledger, and it is a very sizable one, is the creation of the disarmament commission, with the fact that the Assembly, despite the fact that many delegates lacked detailed knowledge of the atomic question, saw through the speciousness of the Soviet arguments for the immediate prohibition of atomic weapons.

In the end, when he realized that all else had failed, Mr. Vishinsky was compelled to submit new proposals that on the surface appeared to be important concessions and conceivably may prove to be so. The debate in the disarmament commission will provide the acid test, but the fact that he felt it necessary to say something new was a sign that the Western powers, under the leadership of the United States, had scored a propaganda victory if nothing else.

There also are grounds for believing that the Western powers scored some points with their proposal for a United Nations survey of the conditions for free elections throughout Germany. On the other hand, the United States lost points by opposing a resolution intended to pave the way for the establishment of a United Nations fund to which the United States would be expected to be the principal contributor—to finance the development of underdeveloped countries.

Although the Assembly rejected Soviet charges that the Mutual Security Act contained a $100 million appropriation for subversive activity in Soviet countries, the United States delegation had great difficulty in defending this indiscretion by Congress and probably lost points. On the other hand despite the losses in Arab and Asian countries, and to some extent in the Latin American countries, the United States' increased support of the colonial powers helped it with the latter, and perhaps this should be scored in the United States' favor.

However, the Security Council election issue was definitely a loss, and so was the United States stand against the Soviet proposal for the bloc admission of fourteen applicants for membership, even though this would have brought in five Communist countries and left South Korea out. The outcome was another Soviet veto of Italy's application, the fifth, and this time Italy and a number of Italy's supporters appeared to hold the United States responsible.

Furthermore, the United States lost more ground by backing to the hilt Nationalist China's charges that the Soviet Union had violated the Soviet-Chinese treaty of friendship of 1945. Even as watered down to state that the Soviet Union had not complied with the treaty, the resolution was carried almost entirely with votes of the United States and its faithful Latin American supporters, the twenty-five abstainers including Britain, France and all the Western European and British Commonwealth countries.

It was inconceivable that these countries would vote with the Soviet Union against the United States, but the abstentions show the extent to which some of the best friends of the United States disapproved of the Chinese Nationalist resolution. Nor were matters improved by the Nationalist representatives' attack on the late President Roosevelt and the Yalta agreement.

In the view of virtually all other delegates the United States position on all three of these losing issues was dictated by the fear of reaction in Congress. Certainly the life of the United States delegates, who are criticized at home for being too soft to communism, and in the United Nations for being too tough, is not a happy one.

Regardless of the wisdom or lack of wisdom of these actions, the tactics used by the United States were criticized by a number of delegates in private conversation. The fundamental objection is the unyielding attitude of the United States on relatively minor matters, which inevitably strengthen Soviet charges of intransigence.

The contrast between the harshness of Secretary of State Dean Acheson's opening speech and that of Anthony Eden, British Foreign Secretary, who was equally firm but used moderate language, was never forgotten. Neither was the obvious hostility in the United States delegation to Mr. Vishinsky's final atomic proposals. Selwyn Lloyd, British Minister of State, said the right thing when, without of course committing his government, he gave the Soviet proposals a warm welcome in the hopes that they would prove real concessions.

Moreover, it would have helped if the United States had revealed one of the principal reasons for its position on membership, the fact that if the Soviet protégés were admitted now, the West would have no leverage left to induce the Soviet Union to agree to the admission of Japan and West Germany later.

Fortunately for the United States, the violence of the Soviet speeches help to make up for some but not all of these mistakes. Moreover, it is a sobering fact that the world-wide commitments of the United States—or as Dr. Philip C. Jessup phrased it, "the fact that we are friends of both parties to several disputes"— inevitably creates difficulties for the United States and Britain.

The Soviet Union does not offer much of a problem in the United Nations now, but it is to be expected that United States leadership will encounter increasing difficulties from other countries at future Assembly sessions. This creates corresponding problems for United States propaganda. The United States was lucky if it got a draw this time.

THE DECLINING INFLUENCE OF THE UNITED STATES [6]

As the Assembly of the United Nations speeded toward adjournment of its Paris sessions the declining influence of the United States in that body became too plain to be mistaken. In the past there has been much talk about this country's "automatic majority" in the UN. So great is our power, and so dependent are many other nations on us for economic and military support, that it has seemed as though this country could command the votes to do whatever it pleased in any of the UN's bodies or agencies. This situation has not wholly changed. And certainly the Soviet Union is no closer to taking over a dominant position in the UN than it has been. Nevertheless, American influence is slipping. On February 1 [1952] this decline jolted the United

[6] From "U.S. Domination in UN Weakening," editorial. *Christian Century*. 69:179. February 13, 1952. Reprinted by permission.

States delegation when the Assembly voted 22 to 21 for a Russian resolution in favor of admitting five Communist and nine non-Communist nations to UN membership, and 25 to 9 for a resolution sponsored by Nationalist China declaring that the Soviet Union had broken its treaty of friendship with China. In both instances, the significant fact was the number of abstentions. In the UN abstention is a way of saying, "I won't vote against you, but I have so many misgivings about what you are doing that I won't vote for you." In the case of the Russian resolution, although the United States managed, under the rule requiring a two-thirds majority for the election of new members, to get one vote more than was needed to block the proposal, 16 nations abstained. And on the resolution branding the Soviet Union a treaty-breaker, there were actually 24 abstentions—within one vote of the number cast in favor! Too much should not be read into these votes. They do, however, reflect a rising anxiety in the UN as to where United States leadership is taking that body and a growing independence on the part of the small nations.

THE UNITED STATES AND COLONIAL POWERS [7]

In an earlier day, when life was much less complicated for the makers of United States policy, the influence of America was exerted automatically on the side of almost any colonial people trying to achieve independence. Americans were very conscious that they had once been under colonial rule themselves, and the spirit of '76 was one of the mainstays of our foreign policy.

This frame of mind, which was shared by President Roosevelt—it is pretty clear that if he had survived the war he would have pressed for the speedy emancipation of the remaining British, French and Dutch colonies—continued to dominate United States policy after the United Nations was established.

Two notable examples in the early postwar period were the strong support given by the United States to the creation of the new states of Israel and Indonesia. Simultaneously the United

[7] From "U.S. Joins Reluctantly with Colonial Powers," by Thomas J. Hamilton, chief of New York *Times* UN Bureau. New York *Times*. p E5. April 20, 1952. Reprinted by permission.

States laid down the policy of favoring discussion of almost any item, including even ridiculous Communist charges against the United States itself, that was presented for inclusion on the agenda of any United Nations organ.

A policy of such Jeffersonian simplicity has now had to give way to the harsh reality of the Soviet menace. That menace made it necessary for the United States to create the North Atlantic Alliance, in which . . . the colonial powers play an indispensable role. And it hardly makes sense to spend billions of dollars providing military and economic help for these partners with one hand, while helping to break up their colonial empires with the other.

This is specially true in the case of such areas as North Africa, which are of such strategic importance that it is vital for the United States to have the right to maintain bases in them against the Soviet threat. . . .

At the same time, the nations that have recently achieved independence, particularly the Arab and Asiatic countries—and even the Latin American countries . . . have come to use the United Nations as an instrument for almost continuous attack on the colonial powers.

Their revolt began in 1949, when they rejected an Anglo-Italian deal regarding the former Italian colonies and voted independence for Libya. It gained strength because of the weakness of Britain and France and the failure of the three great Western powers to work out a common policy.

The choice with which these developments have confronted the United States is not a happy one. At the Paris session of the General Assembly the United States delegation, after painfully obvious hesitation, finally went along with the colonial powers—and with the Latin American countries' delegates who hesitated to make trouble for France while the Assembly was meeting in Paris—in postponing discussion of the complaint against the French administration of Morocco. . . .

The United States, with even greater reluctance, sided with the colonial powers in defeating a similar attempt to place a complaint against the French administration of Tunisia on the agenda of the Security Council. The United States delegation, in fact, made little effort to conceal the fact that it disagreed with the instructions it received from the State Department. . . .

The United States, to be sure, abstained instead of joining France and Britain in voting against discussion of the Tunisian complaint. But, under the Security Council rules, an abstention on such an issue is equivalent to a vote against. Ironically, it was on the insistence of the United States that the Charter prohibited use of the veto over placing an item on the agenda of the Security Council.

It is true enough that the United States vote on Tunisia was no help to our popularity in the Arab and Asiatic countries, and in fact in all countries that are still dominated by their own spirit of '76. But, by the same token, it helped win us friends in most of the NATO countries, which, after all, are those on whom we are placing our principal reliance in our effort to save the free world from totalitarianism. . . .

As far as the interests of the North Africans are concerned, it has been part of the American credo until now that any and all peoples would be better off ruling themselves than being ruled by outsiders, no matter how competent and disinterested outside rule might be. Since it is generally admitted that the Tunisians and Moroccans are far more advanced than the people of Libya, which was granted independence by the United Nations even though it is not and never has been a nation, it may seem hard to justify granting independence to one and withholding it from others.

Nevertheless, if it was a mistake to grant independence to Libya (and to promise it within ten years to Italian Somaliland, which is even more backward), this is no reason to repeat the mistake. And, to judge from the record of some of the Arab governments, there is little reason to expect that the Tunisians and Moroccans would be better off under their own government than they are now.

One thing, however, seems to be clear: If the United States has now been crowded into the position of supporting the colonial powers, that fact gives it a right to use its influence in the interests of effective policy. Recent French policy in both Tunisia and Morocco has been vacillating and ineffective, just as British policy in Iran and Egypt—where the United States, for the same reasons, has supported Britain—has left much to be desired.

It may well be that more intelligent behavior by the colonial powers, if assured the backing of the United States, will guide the present wave of nationalism in both the Mediterranean area and the Far East into more constructive channels. It is more than possible that consistent firmness would have a salutary effect.

Some students of the Egyptian situation are convinced that the anti-British movement would not have been carried to extremes if the Western powers had not tolerated the refusal of Egypt to comply with a Security Council resolution of last summer which called for the removal of Egyptian restrictions on ships passing through the Suez Canal.

Even a perfect policy will not, however, save the colonial powers, and the United States with them, from many brickbats in the United Nations and elsewhere. The situation of the United States is made worse by the fact that the recently liberated countries also are the underdeveloped countries, and the United States has recently lost popularity with them by opposing proposals in the United Nations that all, somehow, envisioned as vast development programs, with the United States footing the bill. . . .

Moreover, the recently liberated countries are ultra-sensitive to any kind of unfavorable comment in newspapers, and they have insisted upon articles in the proposed conventions on freedom of information that the United States opposes because they would actually restrict freedom of information.

It seems fairly clear that United States leadership in the United Nations, which until now has been as unchallenged as British leadership was in the League of Nations, will now have to contend with much greater opposition.

CONSTITUTIONAL CONTROVERSY OVER THE UN [8]

American adherence to various United Nations covenants and conventions, projected with the intent of gaining wider respect

[8] From "Treaties and Domestic Law," by Buel W. Patch, senior research editor. *Editorial Research Reports.* 1, no 13:241-56. March 28, 1952. Reprinted by permission.

for basic rights and fundamental freedoms, is threatened by a rising constitutional controversy in the United States. An important body of opinion holds that the UN multilateral treaties, if ratified by this country, would have the paradoxical effect of endangering full preservation in the United States of the civil liberties whose observance they are designed to promote in other countries. That danger is envisioned primarily in connection with the proposed covenant on human rights and a proposed convention on freedom of information, but the same legal principles are involved in the question of American adherence to the already negotiated genocide convention.

Both the human rights covenant and the freedom of information convention,[9] while setting forth standards to be observed by the signatory states, would permit departures from those standards under certain conditions. Because they would do so, and because the United States Constitution makes treaties the "supreme law of the land," fear has arisen that acceptance of the UN instruments would enable the Federal Government to place restrictions on liberties of American citizens which it otherwise would have no power to impose. There are likewise apprehensions that the genocide convention, by reason of its supremacy as a treaty, would enhance Federal powers at the expense of the states. Although it has been argued that the covenants and conventions would have no such effects on domestic law, particularly in view of the inclusion of provisions aimed specifically to safeguard against that eventuality, the concern not only persists but appears to have increased.

The basis for the contention that the UN pacts hold perils for the United States goes back to that paragraph of Article VI of the Constitution which reads:

> This Constitution, and the laws of the United States which shall be made in pursuance thereof; and all treaties made, or which shall be made, under the authority of the United States, shall be the supreme law of the land; and the judges in every state shall be bound thereby, anything in the constitution or laws of any state to the contrary notwithstanding.

[9] Efforts to complete the freedom of information convention have been suspended for the time being, but the human rights covenant is an active UN project.

The President has the "power, by and with the advice and consent of the Senate, to make treaties, provided two thirds of the
senators present concur" (Article II). Once treaties are signed
and ratified, they have equal validity with the Constitution and
with laws enacted by Congress. The reason for giving treaties
such validity was to avoid any conflict between treaty provisions
and state law. . . .

The constitutional provision which makes treaties the supreme
law of the land as soon as they go into effect is peculiar to the
United States. In most other countries a treaty does not attain
full force as domestic law until made effective by a legislative
act. . . . Although Congress may have to enact legislation to
carry out acts stipulated by a treaty, any self-executing treaty or
part of a treaty automatically attains the status of a statute. . . .

Article VI makes the Constitution, Federal laws enacted "in
pursuance thereof," and treaties all the supreme law of the land.
But Federal laws must conform to the Constitution, and it was
long thought to follow that treaties, occupying the same status
as Federal laws, also must conform. The Supreme Court has
never declared a treaty unconstitutional, but it has frequently
said that it has power to do so. A decision in 1871, for example,
contained the observation that "It need hardly be said that a
treaty cannot change the Constitution or be held valid if it be
in violation of that instrument." . . .

At later decision, however, gave some ground for believing
that a treaty could become an instrument for enhancing Federal
powers; that in this instance Congress, to implement a treaty,
could enact legislation which it would not have power under the
Constitution to enact independently. After a 1913 statute for
protection of migratory birds had been held unconstitutional in
two lower court decisions, the United States in 1916 concluded
a convention on the subject with Canada. To carry out the commitments of the convention, Congress two years later enacted
legislation substantially the same as that enacted in 1913 and
the Supreme Court sustained the new law. . . . The Supreme
Court's opinion in the later case seems to support the theory
that Congress may derive from a treaty powers that it does not
possess under the Constitution. Eberhard Deutsch, a member

of the committee of the American Bar Association which has been studying such questions in connection with the UN covenants has asserted that

> It is only a very short step to a holding that, while Congress and the state legislatures may not, under the provisions of the first and fourteenth amendments to the Federal Constitution, abridge such civil liberties as freedom of speech, press, and assembly, a self-executing treaty or congressional legislation enacted under a treaty dealing with such matters, restricting those liberties, will be upheld as doing no violence to the Constitution.

Defenders of the human rights covenant, seeking to dissipate fears as to its application in the United States, point to one of its articles which states: "Nothing in this covenant may be interpreted as limiting or derogating from any of the rights and freedom which may be guaranteed under the laws of any contracting state or any conventions to which it is a party." . . . The UN covenant, while stating affirmatively that "everyone shall have" the basic rights, would permit such restrictions as are provided by law. . . .

Some practical substance was injected into the controversy over application of the UN multilateral agreements in the United States when a state appeals court in California handed down its decision, April 24, 1950, in the case of Sei Fujii against the State of California. Fujii, a native of Japan resident in California for many years, was appealing from a lower court decision which held that real property which he acquired in 1948 had escheated to the state under a statute which forbade ownership of land by aliens ineligible to citizenship. . . . The appeals court ruled in Fujii's favor on the ground that the restrictions of the land law were "in direct conflict with the plain terms" of the United Nations Charter. . . .

Articles 55 and 56 were the provisions of the Charter on which the court primarily relied to support its decision. Article 55 provides that "the United Nations shall promote," among other things, "universal respect for, and observance of, human rights and fundamental freedoms for all without distinction as to race, sex, language, or religion." Article 56 pledges all member states "to take joint and separate action in cooperation with the (UN) Organization for the achievement of the purposes set forth in Article 55." It is to be noted that Article 56 itself describes the contents of the preceding article as "purposes," and that Article 55 only commits the contracting parties to "promote" achievement of those purposes. That a political commitment of that character could control a court decision on a point of law was something which, in the words of Chairman Connally of the Senate Foreign Relations Committee, the Senate "never dreamed of" when it ratified the Charter.

Manley O. Hudson, Harvard law professor and chairman of the UN's International Law Commission, challenged the whole basis of the California decision. . . . He pointed out that the Charter provisions dealing with human rights and nondiscrimination were no more than statements of purpose which imposed no specific obligation on member nations beyond cooperation. He added that "clearly a court is not the appropriate agency to determine for the government of the United States the particular way in which it should 'cooperate with the United Nations.' " Hudson insisted, moreover, that the Charter provisions "have not been incorporated into the law of the United States because they are not self-executing." As for the Universal Declaration of Human Rights, also cited by the court, it is not a treaty and has no legal force. . . .

Suggestion of such eventualities has led to denunciations of what is called "government by treaty" and "world government through the back door." On the opposite side, the State Department has declared that "our Constitution as the guarantee of our own civil liberties need not and shall not be affected adversely by any international covenant."

OVER-ALL ASSESSMENT OF THE UN [9]

[As to] United Nations accomplishments, potentialities, and shortcomings . . . it is possible to say the following:

(a) Through its peaceful settlement machinery the United Nations has settled or assisted in the settlement of a number of

[9] From "Revision of the United Nations Charter," report of the Senate Committee on Foreign Relations, September 1, 1950. (Senate Report no2501) 81st Congress, 2d session. Superintendent of Documents. Washington, D.C. 1950. p 16-17.

serious disputes, and has halted small conflicts before they could become conflicts of major proportions.

(*b*) As an instrument through which to focus the searchlight of world public opinion on potential aggressors and as a voice for the conscience of the world, the United Nations has acted as an important factor making for peace.

(*c*) Through the purposes and principles of the Charter, and documents like the Declaration on Human Rights, the United Nations has established or is in the process of establishing important standards of conduct for the world community.

(*d*) Through its various organs, the United Nations has enabled the Soviet and non-Soviet worlds to continue to discuss and negotiate with each other concerning mutual problems when other vehicles of communication between them have broken down.

(*e*) The United Nations has given impetus to a new kind of diplomacy in the world of nation states—multilateral diplomacy. Whereas under the more traditional methods of bilateral diplomacy agreements were most frequently made to solve immediate and single issues on the basis of national interests, narrowly conceived, the new diplomacy makes it possible to develop policies both for the simultaneous solution of different issues and for the settlement of single problems in a manner which takes account of the interests of a large number of countries. Furthermore, solutions are likely to be more enduring because they receive direction and focus from the United Nations

(*f*) The economic and social machinery of the United Nations including the specialized agencies, is being used and can be used to coordinate and develop programs for economic and social betterment which will help to remove the causes of war and which will lay the ground work for a more effective international community.

(*g*) Through its authority under Chapter XI of the Charter and through the trusteeship machinery, the United Nations can aid substantially the development of workable solutions to the problems of underdeveloped and dependent areas which otherwise would be likely to act as trouble spots and sources of national rivalry threatening world peace and security.

(*h*) The United Nations, despite its weaknesses, is in all probability a more complete and effective embodiment of the concept of a universal world organization than it would be possible to develop now in view of the deterioration of the international situation since 1945. It is, therefore, a practical basis upon which to build toward more complete and effective international organization.

In this connection it should be pointed out that despite the obstructive tactics of the Soviet Union, especially in the Security Council, the breakdown of the United Nations has been avoided due to the following provisions of the Charter (all opposed, but not voted against, by the Soviet Union at San Francisco):

(1) The wide authority of the General Assembly to deal with all matters relating to the maintenance of peace.

(2) The right of discussion in the Security Council without any great power veto.

(3) The right of collective self-defense under Article 51 of the Charter.

(*i*) Finally, the United Nations serves as a unifying influence. Through acting together in its organs and agencies for the solution of common problems nations and their representatives tend in many instances to gain increased confidence in and understanding of each other. Admittedly a slow process, this aspect of United Nations activity can under a minimum of favorable conditions have the gradual effect of transforming the "one world" concept from theory to actuality.

These positive advantages must, of course, be measured against the question as to how long the organization can survive the increasing pervasiveness and intensity of the ideological struggle for the minds and loyalties of men.

There is no definite answer to such a question. Certainly the present example of the influence of the Soviet walk-out in the United Nations in connection with the failure to seat the Chinese Communist delegate in the Security Council is not encouraging.

While no one can tell as yet what the final outcome will be with respect to the Soviet walk-outs or the seating of the Chinese Communists, it is possible that the new sense of unity which has emerged in the free world as the result of the firm action of the

United Nations in Korea will prevent an undesirable outcome in both cases and give new life to the organization. Certainly it is heartening that an overwhelming majority of members have been ready to endorse action taken by the Security Council to stop aggression.

If the United Nations can get by the present critical period and emerge stronger than ever, and if the Atlantic community continues to gain strength to the degree necessary to act as a real deterrent to Soviet armed action, the usefulness of the organization might be expected to continue and to increase. Even in the present crisis those aspects of United Nations activity not primarily related to the conflict—i.e., economic, social, cultural, and trusteeship aspects—continue to be carried on with a relative degree of effectiveness.

THE UNITED STATES AND REGIONAL SECURITY

EDITOR'S INTRODUCTION

For over a hundred years the Monroe Doctrine has symbolized American foreign policy. This concept of hemispheric unity was the basis of the Good Neighbor policy of the 1930's and even of Herbert Hoover's plea for a "Gibraltar of the West" of 1950 during the Great Debate on foreign policy. Americans have grown up thinking in terms of Western Hemisphere unity and cooperation, even though it is difficult to reconcile this point of view with practical reality. But consistently over the years, official foreign policy announcements have emphasized America's primary interest in the Western Hemisphere.

It is natural, therefore, for American attitudes toward international organization to be governed, in large part, by previous experience with this hemispheric or regional approach to foreign policy. And, in reality, the United States is hardly different from any other nation in this respect. Most major powers have outlined regional plans of one kind or another which envisaged a regional superstate or confederation of states. Usually, of course, the nation most interested saw itself as the dominant power in any such grouping of states. And all too often historical regional pacts were not based on mutual agreement but upon conquest and aggression, such as the united Europe program of Hitler and Mussolini under the label of the Rome-Berlin axis.

The basis for any international grouping of states, through alliances or otherwise, is the desire to achieve something which the individual states are unable to do alone. Naturally, the smaller and weaker nations are the ones most interested in collective security arrangements or other types of international agreements. The primary purpose of such collective pacts has usually been self-defense, for it is only in time of crisis that nations will forgo their sovereign rights for a group goal. And it is naturally far more logical for nations linked by geographic or economic ties to be more interested in association with one another than nations which have few interests in common.

But while these are only common-sense principles of regionalism, the American experience has been based on somewhat different concepts. Political developments within the Western Hemisphere have had no historical parallel in the Old World. While occasional wars between nations have occurred, the Americas have never been torn asunder by the large-scale wars which have engulfed Europe three times in less than ninety years. And participation of American states in Europe's wars has been characterized by one fact: there has been no choosing up of sides so that American states were fighting each other.

So for these reasons, too, it seems natural for Americans to be more concerned with regional organization of a type with which they have had experience than with visionary programs for a world order. It should be noted, however, that while the United States has taken a leading role both in strengthening inter-American organization and in creating and strengthening the world organization, much of the impetus toward hemispheric unity has come from the Latin American nations. Latin leaders have expressed considerable dissatisfaction with the actions of the United States in devoting so much attention to the problems of Europe and Asia, and while they continue to support the United States in the UN they have become increasingly critical of the United States' so-called abandonment of the "American system" in favor of the North Atlantic alliance and other arrangements. They point out somewhat bitterly that American efforts to promote better living conditions through a Point Four Program have almost wholly neglected Latin America—which is also an undeveloped area and is much more important to our national security than far-off lands in the Middle East or South Asia.

In this section an attempt has been made to outline the major developments in American foreign policy which involve regional security arrangements. Seeing the interlocking character of current regional groupings may offer some clue as to what may logically be expected in the future.

THE BASIS OF AMERICAN REGIONALISM [1]

In the closing months of World War II the struggle among United States policy-makers between regionalism and universalism in the approach to international organization came into the open. . . . Supporters of the universalist approach argued that peace in the foreseeable future depended ultimately on the continuance of the wartime coalition of the three powers: Great Britain, the Soviet Union and the United States. The world organization then in formation should be granted as much power as practicably possible. . . .

On the other hand were those who, while sternly repudiating the ostrich-like tendencies of the 1920's, tended to view any world organization as [a] useful backdrop to the strengthening of American ties with specific regions and countries. . . . The second of the policies mentioned has gained almost complete acceptance over the first; although official pronouncements today, like those of 1945, continue in large part to weld the objectives of the first with the actions of the second. Perhaps, therefore, it is not too early to assess in preliminary fashion some of the implications of the choice made or forced upon us in so far as United States relations with the Western Hemisphere are concerned.

The inter-American system as constructed after World War II rests upon three basic instruments. . . . The Act of Chapultepec, signed at Mexico City in 1945; the Inter-American Treaty of Reciprocal Assistance, signed at Quitandinha, Brazil, in 1947; the Charter of the Organization of American States, signed at Bogota in 1948—all contain specific statements of the compatibility between the regional, hemisphere system and the world organization. As such they appear to follow the universalist impulse of American policy and could have served that policy had it even been deemed possible to make it effective. . . .

In the three basic instruments of the inter-American system . . . there was uniformly an asseveration of the consistency of

[1] From "The United States, the Inter-American System and the United Nations," by Edgar S. Furniss, Assistant Professor in Department of Politics of Princeton University. *Political Science Quarterly*. 65:415-30. September 1950. Reprinted by permission.

the regional and the world organizations. . . . The drafters went beyond claims of consistency in an attempt to tie the two organizations together in a functional relationship. This was especially true in the case of collective action to be taken under the Treaty of Reciprocal Assistance. . . . As set forth in the instruments themselves, the relationship appeared to be that of a part to the whole. To put the same idea a little differently, the relationship claimed as existing between the two organizations, was that between one of a number of smaller circles (states and regional systems) embraced by an inclusive circle (the United Nations). The latter was larger than the former and included it together with a number of other integers as well.

When placed in their proper perspective these three instruments can be seen as actually representing the increasing strength of the second, conflicting impulse in American policy.

The Latin American republics came to Mexico City determined (a) that the inter-American system would be strengthened and placed on a sound institutional foundation, and (b) that the world organization as envisaged in the Dumbarton Oaks proposals would not be constructed in such a way as to weaken the regional organization. . . . In so far as the strengthening of the inter-American system was concerned, the United States was an enthusiastic supporter of Latin American desires. . . .

While the inter-American system therefore came potentially strengthened from the Mexico City Conference, the issue of its relation to the emerging world organization was still in doubt. . . . Consequently the issue at San Francisco was basically and in its simplest form whether the regional arrangement or the world organization should have primary power and responsibility for the enforcement of collective security within the region itself. The answer given by the Dumbarton Oaks proposals . . . was clear: primary responsibility was to rest with the world organization. . . .

On the other hand, Latin American desires on this subject, desires supported by the United States, had been made a matter of record in Mexico City. The Act of Chapultepec, it will be remembered, stated that its procedures "shall be consistent with the principles" of the world organization. If the act, already a formally approved document when the San Francisco Conference assembled, should be found to be in conflict with *proposals* for an international organization, consistency would be achieved by modification of the proposals, not of the document.

With the active assistance of members of the United States delegation, Latin American states were successful at San Francisco in reversing the hierarchy of power over enforcement action envisaged in the Dumbarton Oaks proposals to conform to their own previous action at Mexico City. . . .

Now that the shoe was on the other foot the American republics could tighten the hemisphere regional system as much as they pleased, secure in the knowledge that there would be no unwelcome interference from the United Nations. This they proceeded to do. In their successful endeavors they were aided by policy-makers in the United States, among the most prominent of whom were Senators Connally and Vandenberg. . . . Both distinguished senators were staunch advocates of a strong inter-American system. . . .

As written at Rio de Janeiro, therefore, the treaty was an instrument of United States policy and as such enthusiastically endorsed by policy makers in this country. Senator Vandenberg smoothly piloted the treaty through the Senate. . . . The vote on the treaty was overwhelming. . . .

The vote on the treaty must also be interpreted as concrete endorsement of the regional approach to American security, which by the end of 1947 had won all but complete acceptance over the universalist approach. Senator Vandenberg left no doubt as to the primacy of the regional arrangement. It was to the phrases of formal compatibility that he referred when he declared, "This pact is not a substitute for the United Nations. It is a supplement to the United Nations and part of its machinery." But it was to the reality of inter-American exclusive power over collective action within the hemisphere that Vandenberg referred later in the same speech: "The jurisdiction of the 'region' will cease whenever—but not until—'the Security Council has taken the necessary measures to maintain international peace and security' as required in its Charter. I underscore 'necessary measures.' "

Final recognition of the fact that the Rio treaty, together with the charter of Bogota, formed the accepted foundation of the American search for international security was accorded when policy-makers sought to apply the same basic principles to another "region"—the "North Atlantic Community." Scarcely one month after the conclusion of the Bogota conference Senator Vandenberg secured the adoption in the Senate by the decisive vote of 64-4 of the vitally important resolution which bears his name. Reaffirming its faith in the United Nations, the Senate advised the President that it believed the United States should move toward "progressive development of the regional and other collective arrangements for individual and collective self-defense in accordance with the purposes, principles, and provisions of the Charter," and "association of the United States, by constitutional processes, with such regional and other collective arrangements as are based on continuous and effective self-help and mutual aid, and as affect its national security."

There can be no doubt that the close ties forged with Latin America, after the war, inspired the resolution. The State Department made this plain in its own document, issued in the spring of 1949 and entitled *Collective Security in the North Atlantic Area*. The pamphlet begins by citing the Vandenberg Resolution and goes on to correlate the Treaty of Reciprocal Defense with the North Atlantic Pact. . . .

The Charter of the Organization of American States, signed at Bogota, makes the inter-American system as independent of the world organization as it may wish to be. To be sure the members of one are the members of the other; many of the agencies of one are affiliated with agencies of the other. But the American republics have taken the important step of expressly removing all curbs on subjects to be discussed by the system. . . . Should the inter-American system decide to protect itself by action under the treaty, the United Nations would not be able to nullify or to countermand that action. Should the system, on the other hand, prefer to look the other way, the United Nations would perforce do the same thing unless invited to proceed. As guarantor of this independence of the inter-American system stands the veto power which one of its members, the United States, possesses in the Security Council of the United Nations. . . .

At Rio de Janeiro the American states drew in exact geographic terms the line of the inter-American security zone. It stretches from pole to pole and includes Canada, Alaska and Greenland, in addition to a segment of Antarctica. A power attacking the hemisphere from outside that line has, according to the treaty, to reckon with the combined weight of all the American republics. . . .

Thus is the skeletal outline of the gigantic responsibility which the United States has assumed. It alone has the resources materially to aid Latin American economies. It alone has the stability to promote the success of the Organization of American States. It alone has the military strength to preside over the arbitration of inter-American conflict of serious proportions. To this country, then, Latin America must look for action. In such circumstances, with such responsibility, there can be no such thing as a policy of passivity. Anything which the United States does or does not do has a profound effect in Latin America. . . .

American policy derives considerable benefit from the knowledge that the overwhelming majority of Latin American countries will support this country in an emergency. In terms of military security, however, Latin America is a liability, not an asset. . . . The regional arrangements created between the American republics since the war may eliminate one, but by no means all of the dangers to the United States within the locality. (None of the basic instruments of the system are competent to meet the techniques of internal penetration of minds and institutions which is practiced by the Soviet Union.) Nonetheless it should be plain that security within the hemisphere is only part, and a minor one at that, of the type of world security that United States policy seeks. Policy makers well know that the crucial focus of American relations lies in Europe and Asia, not buried in the jungles and mountains of Latin America.

Knowledge, however, is not enough if it is followed by attempts to achieve true world security by the piecemeal application to other so-called regions of the principles applied within the inter-American system. The problems confronted in Europe and Asia are not those to be found in the Western Hemisphere, if only because the individual states on those great continents have had no continued experience with American power and have not been and are not now as defenseless economically, politically, militarily and psychologically as the small Latin American countries. Where the problems are different, the techniques of statecraft must adapt themselves. . . .

It should be fully appreciated that progressive additions of security arrangements with various regions cannot add up to the type of world security which the United States seeks. This concept was basic in the minds of those who sought the establishment of a strong United Nations. The failure to date of the United Nations to operate in the effective manner envisaged by the advocates of the first-mentioned alternate American policy should not lead us to believe that by piling regional blocs on top of one another the United States can easily climb to the apex of world security. Even if the crushing difficulty of defining a "region" for such purposes is ignored, the total is truly infinitely greater than the sum of its parts. In this light such regional arrangements as the United States has made or will make must be viewed, not as ends in themselves but as expedients, enforced means to a greater goal. . . . The end of United States policy can only be the effective operation of a world organization gradually assuming increasing responsibilities.

POPULAR APPEAL OF REGIONALISM [2]

Realizing that they have little influence in a world dominated by the politics of power, the American republics . . . have supported international organization and international law in various forms. . . . Unless it be through some form of international organization, they know that they will have no voice in determining the solutions to the major issues which vitally affect their welfare and the stability of the world.

It is only through some form of international organization, in which the politics of power are subordinated to the procedures

[2] From "The Organization of American States Peace and Power Politics, address before Institute of World Affairs, Riverside, California, December 1951, by Alexander DeConde, Professor of History, Whittier College. *World Affairs Interpreter.* 22:402-14. Winter 1952. Reprinted by permission.

of law, that the Latin American republics, as comparatively insignificant states, can make themselves heard. . . . It is thus not strange that the twenty Latin American nations, together with the United States, have erected the most advanced structure for international peace and security in the world—the Organization of American States. . . .

In the past few years of the "cold war," power politics have threatened the very existence of the United Nations as an instrument of international security. . . . This state of affairs has led to a loss of confidence in the United Nations as *the* instrument for world peace. This loss of confidence, however, has not diminished the appeal of the principles of the United Nations and the hopes of maintaining world peace through some form of international organization. Hence, many men have turned to other international agencies for security, particularly to regional arrangements, even though, oddly enough, the great world ideological split has resolved itself into regional coalitions. The North Atlantic Treaty Organization and the Cominform might well be described as antagonistic regional bodies. There is even a legal basis for this trend toward regionalism. Articles 51, 52, and 53 of the United Nations Charter gave recognition to the existence of regional systems and their place in relation to the world organization. Regional agencies as a result of this recognition are allowed an important role in the vital peace and security system of the United Nations. . . .

Best prepared of the various regional arrangements in the world to take advantage of the Charter provisions was the inter-American system. It gave birth to the oldest, to the most highly integrated, and to the thus far most successful regional organization in the world—the Organization of American States. . . .

Though the Organization of American States is still in its swaddling clothes many a disillusioned supporter of the United Nations, many critics of the world body, and many "hemisphere isolationists," believe the American organization has already established a powerful precedent. To them it beckons as a prototype for regional arrangements and as a kind of logical alternative to the United Nations, without its weaknesses and "dangerous" associations. In many ways it has served as the model for the building of the North Atlantic Treaty Organization. . . .

The position of Senator Taft and other critics [of the UN] poses the question of why the Organization of American States, or the principles behind it, have such great appeal to opponents of the United Nations. . . .

In the first place its appeal is strong because in the disheartening postwar years of the "cold war" it has been the only international organization whose peace machinery has been tested on several occasions and found successful in each test. . . . It has settled a dispute between Costa Rica and Nicaragua in 1948-49. It has resolved another dangerous situation which involved primarily Haiti and Santo Domingo, but which also threatened to entangle Cuba and Guatemala in a four-power war. Though its security powers have been exercised only in dealings with small countries, its accomplishments are nevertheless real and significant. And through these achievements it has gained prestige and has inspired hope for the future.

Secondly, the Organization of American States attracts and holds varied followers because it is not the result of any startling innovations nor does it step on the toes of powerful established interests at home or abroad. It is essentially the practical culmination of ideas and procedures that have long been worked and reworked in the inter-American system. . . . Conservatives can feel at home in this new regional entity because it is, in the main, familiar to them; its innovations are not too radical to alarm them.

Thirdly, the support gained by the Organization of American States from among many Americans may be explained by the fact that it does not suffer from the great-power complex of the United Nations. Within it, power politics are not dominant. . . . There is not here, as there is in the Security Council of the United Nations, an exclusive group of major powers; each American nation is always a member of and participates in every important organ of the Organization of American States. There is also a legal equality of all states in its political mechanics. Each state has one vote of equal weight, and all decisions are made by majority vote. In most cases a two-thirds majority is necessary to carry an issue; in others, only an absolute majority is needed. Such political equality has great appeal for the small powers, especially when contrasted to their position in the United Nations. In this connection, critics of the world organization find the lack of the great power "veto" in the American arrangement singularly praiseworthy.

Lastly, the Organization of American States has, because of its nonintervention provisions which are stronger than those of the United Nations, a great attraction for weak states and those who cherish law above unrestrained force. Only intervention in internal affairs is prohibited by the United Nations. The American Charter, however, has been set up to prohibit all intervention, whether external or internal, the only exception being measures taken to enforce peace under the provisions of the Rio treaty. . . .

It might truthfully be said that the Organization of American States is an instrument of power politics. But, unlike Soviet satellites, it is a voluntary participant in the world struggle. It makes its power felt through lawful procedures, not as a result of knuckling down to force.

By thus assuming a share in world responsibilities, the Organization of American States may avoid falling into the trap of regional isolationism. This is a real danger. For many of the ardent supporters of the American regional system would most like to see it become a vehicle for a new hemisphere isolationism. The past reveals that the Latin American states as well as the United States have a record of isolationism. Today, of all the American states, it is only the United States that is a true world power. Consequently, the world situation affects the Organization of American States primarily through the influence it exerts on the United States. Hence the role of this new body of American states as a mechanism for peace must be understood in the light of the world situation of which it is a part and not in terms of an isolated regional entity. . . .

The position of the Organization of American States in the world is unique. It is a body of twenty weak states and one superstate. . . . The very fact of its uniqueness indicates that much that makes for success in the Organization of American

States would not work for other regional arrangements. Other groups could profit from its experience and might even be able to adopt some of its machinery. But beyond this, its limitations are marked. The very essence of regionalism is an adaptation to local needs and a recognition of regional peculiarities. It is difficult to see, under these circumstances, how it could serve as a beacon model for a world movement toward regionalism.

Within the limits of its functions the Organization of American States has demonstrated a successful application of the powers of peace and law in one area of the world. Beyond this one special area, its powers are limited. Despite its obvious success thus far, its basic structural improvements for collective security and its bright hope for the future, the Organization of American States should not be looked to as a substitute for the United Nations. It is the United Nations which is entrusted, in a much too limited way, with the responsibilities for world peace. A peace without fear is an indivisible peace and cannot be brought about piecemeal through regional organizations, often with diverse and opposing interests. The problems of power politics and world peace, in the long view, can probably be settled only by a strong universal international organization, aided, not subverted, by regional systems. But, above all, it must be understood that the Organization of American States, the United Nations, or any other international organization will not bring in the millenium. The best that can be expected of any international body is a laborious, heartbreaking struggle, beset by trial and error, toward the goal of peace and security for most men in the world, but perhaps never for all.

CONGRESS AND THE REGIONAL APPROACH [3]

The Vandenberg resolution (Senate Resolution 239, 80th Congress) which was passed by the Senate had two aspects. First, the Senate advised that certain specific objectives should be sought within the existing United Nations structure. Second,

[3] From "Revision of the United Nations Charter," report of the Senate Committee on Foreign Relations, September 1, 1950. (Senate Report no2501) 81st Congress, 2d session. Superintendent of Documents. Washington, D.C. 1950. p20-2.

the Senate suggested the development of "regional and other collective arrangements for individual and collective self-defense" which, while permitted by the Charter, were, if not outside the Charter, at least alongside the Charter. The two aspects of the Vandenberg resolution were rooted in the fundamental purpose of the Charter "to maintain international peace and security" but they pointed to different roads which might be followed to reach that goal. One might be described as the "regional" or "collective defense" route, the other as the "universal" or "Charter" route. If the Charter route failed because of Soviet road blocks or detours, to lead to international peace and security, the collective-defense detour might in time lead the free nations to the same destination and might also provide a means of opening the Charter route.

The United States Government has been sending its task forces along both roads. The most striking movements toward peace and security in the past three years have been along the road of collective self-defense. The difficulties which the United Nations has encountered because of the obdurate attitude of the Soviet Union has caused the United States and other free nations more and more to seek peace and security along this road. . . .

The Rio pact was in a sense a projection of the Monroe Doctrine and the inter-American system. . . . It . . . provided machinery for collective action against armed attack or aggression in the Western Hemisphere from within or without. . . . The North Atlantic Treaty . . . was signed in April 1949. It reaffirmed the faith of the signatories in the purposes and principles of the Charter, it pledged the members to act consistently with these purposes and principles, it provided that action taken under the treaty should be reported to the United Nations Security Council and that such action was to cease when the Security Council had taken measures necessary to maintain peace and security. . . . The principal undertaking was recognition that an armed attack against one of the members was to be viewed as an attack against all and in that event each member was to take such action as it deemed necessary to restore and maintain security. . . .

As a further step in implementing the North Atlantic Treaty and in developing an effective collective defense arrangement within the purview of, but supplementary to, the Charter, the Congress passed the Mutual Defense Assistance Act of 1949 . . . [which] read in part as follows:

The Congress hereby finds that the efforts of the United States and other countries to promote peace and security in furtherance of the purposes of the Charter of the United Nations require additional measures of support based upon the principle of continuous and effective self-help and mutual aid. These measures include the furnishing of military assistance essential to enable the United States and other nations dedicated to the purposes and principles of the United Nations Charter to participate effectively in arrangements for individual and collective self-defense in support of those purposes and principles.

The mutual defense effort of the North Atlantic Treaty signatories is but the most recent of a number of formal and informal acts indicating that in the North Atlantic there is a community of interest that goes beyond the concept of the regional pact. . . . The developing Atlantic community is consistent with the principles and purposes of the United Nations Charter, but is outside the Charter. As members of the United Nations support the Charter in their international relations, one with the other or on a multilateral basis as in the Atlantic community, the United Nations will be strengthened.

THE PROBLEM OF NATO VERSUS UN [4]

The Palais de Chaillot annex in Paris, which was built last summer with such speed and enthusiasm for the 1951 session of the United Nations General Assembly, has now been taken over by the Secretariat of the North Atlantic Treaty Organization.

Some [UN] delegates . . . think that the fact that NATO has moved into the Assembly's Paris headquarters is more than a mere symbol. The responsibility for law and order in the most important area of the world has clearly passed from the United Nations to the North Atlantic Treaty countries. The question . . .

[4] From "NATO Assuming the Place UN Was Expected to Fill," by Thomas J. Hamilton, New York *Times* chief of UN Bureau. New York *Times.* p E5. April 27, 1952. Reprinted by permission.

is whether NATO, which was intended to be only a temporary safeguard against aggression, will eventually supersede the United Nations.

Already, of course, the United Nations of today has ceased to bear much resemblance to the United Nations that was dreamed of when the Charter was written at San Francisco seven years ago. . . .

The really melancholy fact, from the viewpoint of the United Nations, is that the world is now looking to NATO, and to the mutual defense treaties between the United States and Australia, New Zealand, the Philippines and Japan for effective defense against any new Communist aggression.

Regional security agreements were, of course, authorized by Article 51 of the United Nations Charter, which safeguarded the inherent right of individual and collective self-defense against armed attack. However, the Charter also made it clear that the United Nations was to be a world-wide instrument of collective security, and that any regional arrangements that might have to be made should be entirely temporary.

A considerable number of delegates, however, accept the United States contention that NATO was intended to strengthen the United Nations, not to by-pass it. And probably all members of the United Nations, except for the Soviet-controlled or neutralist delegates agree that, whether or not NATO has weakened the United Nations, the Soviet menace left the United States with no alternative.

The difficulty is that these same delegates know that, as far as public opinion in both the United States and in other free countries is concerned, the United Nations now plays a secondary role to NATO. The slowly increasing total of divisions that would be available against a Soviet attack on Western Europe is added up in terms of NATO; forecasts of what would happen in the Far East if either of the Communist great powers began an attack take little notice of the United Nations and concentrate on the efficacy of America's bilateral treaties with the island nations of the Pacific. . . .

Neither the United States nor any of the principal democratic powers has pledged itself to place armed forces at the disposition of the Assembly. Greece and the Philippines are the only countries with any sizable number of troops who have done so. There now appears to be little prospect that the Assembly will ever have a sort of standing army at its disposal, in the same way that the Security Council was intended to have one—although it never actually did.

On the other hand, even though an effective force were obtained, the decision to use it would, of course, have to be taken by majority vote—and year after year the movement against the colonial powers is gaining strength in the United Nations. Apart from the five members of the Soviet bloc, the Arab and Asiatic countries and to a lesser extent the Latin American countries, are now so hostile to the colonial powers that it may be doubted whether they would vote for United Nations action even if Communist China intervened openly in Indo-China, the most likely source of new trouble if there is an armistice in Korea. It is possible that enough of them would abstain to make possible the needed two-thirds majority in the Assembly, but even so such a resolution would have little moral effect.

Even assuming that the necessary military force was available, and that the Assembly could be depended upon to use it on the right side, a number of Western European delegates believe that it would be better to depend upon regional agreements against aggression rather than upon the United Nations. Arguing from the Korean experience, they contend that such Assembly resolutions as those condemning Communist China as an aggressor, and imposing an embargo on strategic materials have already threatened to widen the conflict, and that similar action in the future might convert a limited war into a world war. They believe the United Nations should be kept in reserve to help settle conflicts, or, if the worst happens, to make peace after another world war.

These diverse and partly contradictory arguments seem to point to one conclusion: under present circumstances effective action against any future aggression will be taken, if it is taken at all, through regional defense arrangements.

EISENHOWER REPORT: NATO'S FIRST YEAR [5]

There is no real security yet achieved in Europe; there is only a beginning.

Equally, it would be unfortunate . . . to find excuse for defeatism in the manifold difficulties and shortcomings of our joint effort to date. For we have made progress in all aspects of security. . . .

NATO itself is a significant step to meet both the present danger of aggression and the tragic struggles and dissensions that have divided our peoples in the past. But NATO's development is not automatic: action is the test.

To advance this great effort, unified action is required, not only among but within our nations. . . .

The unity of NATO must rest ultimately on one thing—the enlightened self-interest of each participating nation. The United States, for example, is furnishing much of the material resources of this project during the current year because it believes that America's enlightened self-interest is served thereby. Most American people agree as to the wisdom and necessity of this course. But they will continue to believe their own security interests are being served only as other participants show cooperation and enterprise in improving their own defenses.

Consequently, it would be fatuous for anyone to assume that the taxpayers of America will continue to pour money and resources into Europe unless encouraged by steady progress toward mutual cooperation and full effectiveness. . . .

Fundamentally, and on a long-term basis, each important geographical area must be defended primarily by the people of that region. The average citizen must therefore feel that he has a vital stake in the fight for freedom, not that he is a bystander or a pawn in a struggle for power. There is so much talk of national and international arrangements and interests that basic issues are often obscured from view. . . .

[5] From "Text of Eisenhower's First Annual Report to NATO as Commander of West's Forces," by General Dwight D. Eisenhower. New York *Times*. p 14-15. April 2, 1952.

By our actions, too, we must demonstrate in convincing form that we are masters of our own destiny. Within the Atlantic community and in Europe, we have the opportunity to build a bulwark of peace—a central position of unity and strength for the free world. This, then, must be a first and fundamental consideration. . . . One year ago it was clear that the difficulties facing the new enterprise were manifold. . . It is common knowledge that peacetime coalitions throughout history have been weak and notoriously inefficient. Sovereign nations have always found it difficult to discover common ground on which they could stand together for any length of time. Nevertheless, we were expecting NATO members not only to agree on common objectives but to work and sacrifice together, over an indefinite period, in order to achieve common security.

The United States, aided by other members of the United Nations, was already heavily engaged in combat operations in Korea which were taking a severe toll in manpower and military supplies. Moreover, strong voices could be heard in America, disputing the NATO concept of collective security and opposing a further United States reinforcement of the European area. France was engaged against aggression in Indo-China in a bitter struggle that absorbed a large portion of her regular military establishment.

This campaign in southeast Asia was already draining off a significant share of the money and resources that the French Government could allocate to military purposes, even though the United States was providing assistance in the form of aircraft, tanks, and heavy equipment. In Malaya, British forces, equivalent to more than two divisions, were engaged against guerrilla activities inspired by Communist agents.

There was serious question as to the state of public morale among the European members of the North Atlantic Treaty Organization. They were living daily under the shadow of a powerful Soviet striking force, stationed in Eastern Germany and Poland, and possessing the obvious capability of overrunning much of Europe. It was extremely difficult for the average European to see any future in an attempt to build defensive forces which might offset this real and formidable threat. There seemed to be too much of a lead to be overtaken.

The doubts of the European peoples gave birth to the false but glittering doctrine of neutralism, through which they hoped to preserve the things they had always held dear. Their fears were stimulated by ugly overtones of threat from Communist propaganda organs and from traitorous outriders already in their own midst. . . .

These were only a few of the obvious obstacles in the road leading to the collective security of the still free world. . . . The effect of the negative factors was largely canceled by a stern fact which denied refutation: the job had to be done. . . . There was no acceptable alternative. Otherwise, nation after nation, beginning with the weaker and the more exposed, would be infiltrated, harassed and browbeaten into submission. . . .

If the continued advance of the Iron Curtain could eventually damage the economic and therefore the political system of America, how much more critical was the position of practically every other nation exposed to the threat. Truly there could be no question on the part of any member of the North Atlantic Treaty Organization as to the overriding need for joint and vigorous defense action. Without it there was, in long-term sense, hope for none. . . .

To assist free nations, in Europe and elsewhere, to build their own defenses against the persistent threat of aggression, the United States inaugurated the Mutual Defense Assistance Program late in 1949. The purpose of this program was to furnish items of military equipment which the other countries could not produce, and to assist in the training required for the effective use of those weapons. In the European area, the program also provided the countries some of the machine tools, materials and various components needed to get the production of munitions started. . . .

Despite this extensive aid, the rearmament program meant heavy budget increases in all European countries. . . .

The effect of defense spending on national economies was greatly magnified by sharp world-wide increases in the cost of raw materials. Food, coal, and other basic necessities soared to new heights, kindling antagonism against governmental defense programs and the whole rearmament effort. . . .

However, the concerted effort toward greater strength made progress throughout the spring and summer months. The attitude of the governments was cooperative, but there did exist a general feeling that an accurate yardstick was needed within NATO to measure the scale and intensity of national effort. Obviously, this was an extremely complicated problem in view of the differences in natural resources, financial position, industrial potential, and standards of living of various nations. Yet, failure to meet the situation would eventually lead to dissatisfaction and friction among our membership. . . .

Concern was felt in many quarters over the apparent failure to put to full use existing production facilities of Europe. . . .

Recognition of the specific problems impeding progress led to the appointment of the Temporary Council Committee at the NATO meeting in Ottawa during September of 1951.

The primary task of the TCC was to develop a plan of action reconciling the issues arising from an acceptable military program with the actual capabilities of member countries. . . . In the process, the committee surveyed the political and economic capabilities of each NATO country, as well as problems requiring attention in order to develop these capabilities. . . .

The operation of the committee was truly an innovation in that sovereign nations permitted an international group to examine their defense programs and their capacity—financial, economic and military—of supporting heavier burdens.

As a result, the true dimensions of the rearmament task could be seen for the first time in terms of an integrated military, economic, and financial effort. . . .

Even with the maximum potential realized through the collective efforts of member nations, there is little hope for the economical long-term attainment of security and stability in Europe unless Western Germany can be counted on the side of the free nations. Here in the heart of Europe is an area of roughly 100,000 square miles populated by nearly 50,000,000 industrious and highly skilled people. Rich in natural resources and production facilities, Western Germany alone produces one-half as much steel annually as the rest of Western Europe combined. . . .

As the geographic center of Europe, Western Germany is of great strategic importance in the defense of the Continent. The northern plain of Germany, with its extensive network of modern roads and railways, offers the best route of advance from the East. As of today, our forces could not offer prolonged resistance east of the Rhine barrier. Thus we might lose, by default, the considerable resources of Germany and suffer, at the same time, direct exposure of Denmark and the Netherlands.

With Western Germany in our orbit, NATO forces would form a strong and unbroken line in central Europe from the Baltic to the Alps. . . .

Recognizing the importance of German participation, the United States proposed to the North Atlantic Council in the fall of 1950 that a plan be devised to obtain a German contribution to Western European defense within the framework of NATO. At Brussels in December 1950, the various aspects of this proposal were studied by members of the Council, who then invited the United States, the United Kingdom and France to discuss the matter with the German Federal Republic.

Meanwhile, the French Government proposed an appealing innovation: why not, they said, bring the Germans in as part of a unified European defense force? For several years, France had been a leader in promoting unity in Europe and was, at the time, negotiating the Schuman Plan, a major expression of economic unity. It was felt that German participation within the framework of a European defense community would not only provide the safeguards desired by Germany's neighbors of the West, but would represent also a major step toward European federation. In this spirit, France met with Italy, Belgium, Luxembourg, and Western Germany to evolve an acceptable formula for German participation. From these meetings the concept of a European defense force emerged.

No one has attempted to minimize the difficulty of the new and complex problems implicit in such a plan. On the contrary, the doubters and the critical have magnified these in the hope of halting progress. Partial loss of sovereignty, complexity in administration and maintenance, destruction of patriotic impulse, and dozens of other valid and invalid objections have been plead as establishing the futility of the proposal. Here, as in so many others of the arguments developing around NATO, the answer is found in a simple test. It is: "If this plan is not adopted, what is the inevitable result on the peace and the security we seek to preserve?" . . .

As presently conceived, the European defense force calls for the pooling of forces into a common military organization for the defense of all. Initially, the forces to be unified would be those allocated by the participating nations to the defense of Europe. Troops required to meet commitments outside of Europe proper would be retained under national control. The direction, support, and administration of the unified defense forces would be vested in a European defense community, including a European assembly, a council, a court of justice, and an executive group, along with agencies for military supply, procurement, and budget. Such integration of military forces, and particularly the integration of supply and supporting agencies, would prevent any participating nation from embarking on a separate course of aggression. . . .

When formed, the European defense force would be integrated under SHAPE in the same manner as purely national forces from the United States, Canada, the United Kingdom, and other countries not members of the European defense community. The new grouping would not modify, conflict with, or in any way supersede the North Atlantic Treaty Organization. The concept of a European defense force is the consolidation of military elements of five nations of the North Atlantic Treaty Organization with forces from still another nation, Western Germany. It cannot fail to increase greatly the effectiveness of our collective security and to facilitate the achievement of NATO aims. . . .

Such efficiency demands the closest kind of political and economic cooperation, particularly in the area of Western Europe. For if the free nations of this region were really a unit, tremendous benefits would accrue to them individually and to NATO. Few Europeans would quarrel with this concept: political and economic unity is a popular theme to millions who have suffered from past differences. Yet progress toward full cooperation has been limited by the intricate and artificial maze of national obstacles erected by man himself. Customs barriers, conflicting economic structures, currency regulations, and countless other road blocks curtail drastically the movement of men, manufactured products, raw materials, and money upon which Europe's economic life depends. They are expensive and wasteful encumbrances, pyramiding the cost of production with tariffs, overhead, taxes, and middlemen. In the political field, these barriers compound inefficiency with distrust and suspicion.

[In Europe today] the advantages of political and economic unity can be demonstrated by such practical examples as the European defense force and the Schuman Plan, which embrace the same six countries. The Schuman Plan calls for the pooling and production of steel and coal—vital commodities of life and defense. The aim is to provide common objectives and common markets, to eliminate unreasonable customs barriers, to make the European economy more flexible and productive.

"This plan to work together in steel and coal is, with the European defense community, a promise of greater economic, military, and moral strength in Western Europe. It is tangible evidence of the desire to eliminate the weaknesses of separate little economies, which make it hard for Europe to arm for defense. . . . The two plans, the Schuman Plan and the European defense community, mark historic advances in European cooperation. If these could be supplemented by a Schuman plan for electric power and for agriculture, along with a system for standardizing money values, the benefits would be profound and far-reaching. These joint efforts would serve as practical laboratories for the development of that full political and economic unity which alone can make Europe self-sustaining and secure. Indeed, until this hope becomes an accomplished fact, or some miracle brings about a disappearance of the Soviet threat, there will be no confident peace and enlarging prosperity for any part of the free world.

Although it is my conviction that a unified Europe offers the best hope for permanent stability in this critical area, respectable strength can nevertheless be achieved within NATO by wholehearted effort and cooperation. Much has been done toward that end in the past twelve months. . . . Should the tragedy of another war occur, the sweep of combat will be over broader and deeper areas. Thus the zone of battle, in its three dimensions, will tend to expand, and every element contributing directly to the conduct or support of military operations will become a target for enemy action. The concept of the maintenance of national military forces by states of small geographical extent has already become outdated. The logic of larger groups and association is becoming increasingly impelling. In the NATO nations, especially, the resultant task is to reconcile the demands for association into larger groupings with the deep and spiritual ties to nationhood and sovereignty. . . . As months have passed, confidence has grown throughout the NATO community from the existence of greater and more effective forces and an organization to direct and support them. However, we have not yet succeeded in bringing the full force, the full moral potential of our freedom-loving peoples into the stark struggle for survival of priceless values.

Our goals are simple; they are honorable; they can be achieved. Why, therefore, should there be confusion in the minds of millions of our own peoples as to the basic aims of our defense program, the necessity for it, and the urgent demand for their own individual efforts? Once these facts are established in the minds of our Atlantic peoples, there will be less bickering in our councils, and it will become progressively more difficult for self-seeking individuals to delay our progress by exploiting internal national divisions or minor grievances between our members. . . .

The tide has begun to flow our way and the situation of the free world is brighter than it was a year ago. At Lisbon, our member nations made great headway on issues vital to our continued progress. They strenthened our eastern flank by bringing into NATO the stout-hearted peoples of Greece and Turkey. They agreed to the concept of a European defense community and a close relationship with the German Federal Republic. They approved a program to establish this year a force of fifty standing and reserve divisions and four thousand aircraft.

When combined with the ready strength available in Greece and Turkey, this force—if properly armed and trained—should produce an encouraging degree of security. . . .

There is power in our union—and resourcefulness on land, sea and air. Visible and within grasp we have the capability of building such military, economic, and moral strength as the Communist world would never dare to challenge. When that point is reached, the Iron Curtain rulers may finally be willing to participate seriously in disarmament negotiations. Then, we may see fulfilled the universal hope expressed in the United Nations Charter to reduce "the diversion for armaments of the world's human and economic resources." Then the Atlantic community will have proved worthy of its history and its God-given endowments. We shall have proved our union the world's most potent influence toward peace among men—the final security goal of humanity.

PACIFIC REGIONAL PACTS [6]

The United States has now signed four major treaties with Pacific nations. One of these is the Treaty of Peace between forty-eight Allied powers and Japan. The other three are security treaties, one with the Philippines, another with Australia and New Zealand and the third with Japan.

The Treaty of Peace with Japan has two great purposes. It is first of all designed to close an old war on terms which will not provoke another war. . . . Second and even more difficult . . . was to translate Japan from a defeated enemy into a positive contributor to collective security in the Pacific as against the new menace of aggression which had arisen even before the old war was formally ended.

Japan's strategic position and her human and industrial potential are such that there can be no adequate security for anyone in the West Pacific unless the Japanese sincerely desire to be sustaining members of the free world. That, happily, is now the case. . . .

[6] From "Security in the Pacific," by John Foster Dulles, special representative of the President in charge of negotiating the Japanese Peace Treaty and the Pacific security treaties. *Foreign Affairs*, 30:175-87. January 1952. Reprinted by permission.

The Treaty of Peace contemplates that Japan will promptly apply for membership in the United Nations, and each of the forty-four United Nations members who signed the treaty can be counted on to support that application. However, delays may intervene . . . so Japan undertakes . . . "to give the United Nations every assistance in any action it takes in accordance with the Charter and to refrain from giving assistance to any state against which the United Nations may take preventive or enforcement action."

In return, the Allied powers . . . recognize that Japan, "as a sovereign nation possesses the inherent right of individual or collective self-interest . . . and that Japan may voluntarily enter into collective security agreements." . . .

As a result of these peace treaty provisions, Japan, although not yet a member of the United Nations, will cooperate in any UN action of a preventive or enforcement character and will in important ways contribute "facilities, including rights of passage, necessary for the purpose of maintaining international peace and security." Also, Japan gains the right to collective self-defense, so that, though now disarmed, she need not be a vacuum of power which would attract aggression.

By making its bilateral treaty with the United States, Japan at once exercises her right of collective self-defense. Under this treaty, United States sea, air and land forces and Japanese facilities will be combined for the maintenance of international peace and security in the Far East and for the security of Japan. . . .

At the same time that it was negotiating peace with Japan, the United States also negotiated security treaties with Australia and New Zealand and with the Philippines. These two security treaties are much alike. The parties to each treaty declare that "an armed attack in the Pacific area on any of the parties would be dangerous to its own peace and safety." This language goes back to the classic language of the Monroe Doctrine. It differs from the language of the North Atlantic Treaty which provides that "an armed attack against one . . . shall be considered an attack against them all." . . .

Both the security treaty with Australia and New Zealand and the mutual assistance treaty with the Philippines bind the parties, in accordance with the Vandenberg resolution, "separately and jointly by means of continuous and effective self-help and mutual aid" to "maintain and develop their individual and collective capacity to resist armed attack."

The United States-Philippine treaty is primarily significant in converting a unilateral relationship into one of mutuality. The historic relationship between the peoples of the Philippines and of the United States is such that, as President Truman said in his statement of April 18, 1951, "the whole world knows that the United States recognizes that an armed attack on the Philippines would be looked upon by the United States as dangerous to its own peace and safety and that it would act accordingly." However, the time had come to put that relationship into a treaty of mutuality, which would be responsive to the dignity of the Philippines' newly attained sovereignty.

Both the Australia-New Zealand and Philippine treaties define an armed attack to include an attack upon any land under the jurisdiction of the parties in the Pacific and also an attack on its "armed forces, public vessels or aircraft in the Pacific." For the purposes of the treaties, then, there would be an armed attack on the United States if there were an armed attack upon Okinawa, which the United States is administering, or an attack on the American armed forces stationed in or about Japan under the security treaty with that country. In this practical sense the three security treaties and the Japanese peace treaty interlock.

From our standpoint, the arrangements which we have been considering add up to a determination—with the concurrence and help of the peoples concerned—to make safe the offshore island chain which swings south through Japan, the Ryukyus, the Philippines, Australia and New Zealand. In addition the President has declared that the United States will not permit the status of Formosa, now the seat of the national government of China, to be changed by force, and the Pacific Fleet has been instructed accordingly. That sum total is an impressive development of United States policy and a formidable deterrent to the domination of the Pacific by Communist imperialism. It may be asked why the result has been brought about by a series of separate treaties, rather than by a single treaty. . . .

There were several reasons against doing that. A present reason . . . is that the Australian, New Zealand and Philippine peoples have memories of Japanese aggression which are so vivid that they are reluctant to create a mutual security pact which will include Japan. . . .

It is not at this time practicable to draw a line which would bring all the free peoples of the Pacific and East Asia into a formal mutual security area. . . . The future of Korea, as an independent, united and free nation, is obscure, and there is need for further United Nations action before Korea could be brought into a regional security pact. Those Asian nations such as Indonesia and Burma which have just won liberation from Japanese aggression and political freedom from Western colonialism have hesitated to assume security relationships either with Japan or with the Western powers. As a practical matter, in Indo-China and Malaya assistance must be given largely through France and the United Kingdom, a procedure which many in Asia find repellent, as promoting "colonial imperialism." Some countries are as yet unable or unwilling to qualify for definite security arrangements under the "Vandenberg formula" of "continuous and effective self-help and mutual aid." Lastly, but perhaps not least, is the fact that the United States should not assume formal commitments which overstrain its present capacities and give rise to military expectations we could not fulfill, particularly in terms of land forces. The security treaties now made involve only islands, where security is strongly influenced by sea and air power.

All of the parties to the present Pacific security treaties have, however, made it clear that they do not regard the present situation as adequate or final. The Australia-New Zealand treaty and the Philippine treaty both refer to "the development of a more comprehensive system of regional security in the Pacific area." The United States-Japan security treaty is not only described as "provisional" but it will expire when "there shall have come into force such United Nations arrangements or such alternative individual or collective security dispositions as will satisfactorily provide for the maintenance by the United Nations or otherwise of international peace and security in the Japanese area."

But treaty words in themselves have little power to compel action. Treaties of alliance and mutual aid mean little except as they spell out what the people concerned would do anyway.

The Rio pact reflected a sense of common destiny as between the Americas which had existed for 125 years before it was formalized. The North Atlantic Treaty reflected a sense of common destiny as between the peoples of the West, which grew out of a community of race, religion and political institutions, and it had been tested in two world wars before it was formalized. The security treaties which we have now made with Australia, New Zealand, the Philippines and Japan reflect the fact that the historical events of the recent past have developed a sense of common destiny between our nation and each of those others. But that element does not clearly exist as yet elsewhere in the Pacific area.

AMERICAN INTEREST IN EUROPEAN INTEGRATION

EDITOR'S INTRODUCTION

Viewed in the light of regional organization, the increasing effort on the part of the United States to effect some sort of European unification becomes more understandable. While the immediate aim is one of military expediency, the whole pattern of American-European collaboration tends more and more toward political and economic integration as well. While the United States has always prided itself on never meddling in the internal affairs of foreign nations, the inability of Europe to get on its feet economically after World War II produced a contrary reaction on the part of many Americans. Originally, the United States looked upon efforts toward European integration "with sympathy" but took no direct measures to encourage such action. But as billions in foreign aid produced few if any permanent results, American leaders came to realize that Europe couldn't recover without taking extraordinary measures. But while everyone became firmly convinced of the necessity for some kind of European integration to offset the many barriers between nations, there was considerable disagreement as to the direction this integration should take.

The problems and complexities involved in attempts to unify Europe, whether economically or politically, provide a striking insight into the problems of any international organization or federation on a large scale. Accustomed to think primarily in terms of the generally consistent harmony of the American states, it was a shock to many Americans to find so much disharmony in and among European nations. Britain favored close collaboration with Europe, but no firm political ties—pleading prior commitments with her Commonwealth. Scandinavia showed little interest in any continental arrangement of any sort, saying flatly that their countries much preferred stronger ties with Britain and America. France feared Germany, the Netherlands feared lowering of her standard of living to a common European level. So while tremendous progress has been made toward unification, the outcome is still in doubt. And in the UN non-European nations, even including the Latin American states, question whether a united Europe wouldn't tend to weaken the UN and threaten the security of small nations formerly dominated by the major colonial powers.

While the question has not yet been raised in the United States, the power of a unified Europe in the field of world trade could easily create many new problems. Since to buy from the United States, Europe must export to the United States, an economic federation would be in a much stronger bargaining position to trade on more favorable terms. And whereas the United States thinks largely in terms of free, unrestricted trade, Europe has long seen the advantages of a regulated trade, favoring cartels and currency manipulation to offset trade inequalities.

So while it is temporarily expedient for the United States to urge a strong, united Europe able to defend herself against Communist aggression, it should be considered whether such a strong regional grouping would be desirable in the long run. And we also need to consider how an "integrated Europe" will fit into the pattern of a world organization.

EUROPEAN INTEGRATION AND UNITED STATES POLICY [1]

In previous centuries plans for uniting Europe were in effect plans for creating a world government, for Europe was not only the major arena of world politics but the home of all of its chief actors. In our own day Europe remains the major arena but the traditional great powers are no longer the chief actors. Europeans may much more readily feel that only a Europe united can regain control over its own destiny.

Certainly in no previous period has the idea of European unity received the support of so many political leaders represent-

[1] From "Western European Integration," in *United States—Western Europe Relationships as Viewed Within the Present Worldwide International Environment*, a compilation of discussion materials, by the American Assembly. The Assembly, Graduate School of Business, Columbia University. New York. 1951. p69-77. Reprinted by permission.

ing so many different political viewpoints. . . . However, the federalist pleas that Western Europe will find more peace, strength, and prosperity in unity than in division have not been the sole impetus to postwar "integration" in Europe. A stronger motive force has been provided by the presence of concrete problems whose very nature challenged a concerted, cooperative approach to their solution. Even before the war's end, European nations had combined with others to tackle the tasks of postwar relief and rehabilitation, as well as the longer-range problems of economic reconstruction. Some of these plans—like UNRRA [United Nations Relief and Rehabilitation Administration] or the Bretton Woods agencies were on a global scale; others were European in scope (for example, the emergency agencies of 1945-47: European Coal Organization, European Emergency Economic Committee, European Central Inland Transport Organization).

When it appeared by early 1947 that the initial plans had gravely underestimated the magnitude of the task of postwar reconstruction and that a "second wind" was needed to avert imminent crisis, a new potent stimulus was provided for cooperative European action. Such action was strongly encouraged by the United States, which made its aid to European recovery conditional upon cooperative self-help.

A further challenge to unite—and the most powerful of all—was provided by the growing sense of the Soviet-Communist threat to the basic political order of Europe.

Western Europe . . . responded to the twin challenge of economic crisis and communism. Seventeen governments joined forces in the Organization for European Economic Cooperation, (OEEC) to attack the pressing problems of inadequate production, the dollar gap and inflation. Five nations formed a military alliance in the Brussels Treaty, later to be expanded, under United States leadership, into the North Atlantic Treaty Organization (NATO).

Two strains are thus discernible in Western Europe's movement towards unity. There is what may be called the political or federalist approach, which strives to establish new supra-national organs of European government, to which the component nations would formally surrender parts of their sovereign rights.

The Strasbourg agencies exemplify this striving. There is, on the other hand, a trend towards concerted intergovernmental action on concrete tasks: as exemplified by OEEC in the economic realm and NATO in that of military defense. This approach—which "pools" sovereignties and to that extent accomplishes genuine cooperative action in certain specific fields is often styled the "functional" method of integration. . . .

The insistence with which American foreign policy in recent years has played the theme of European integration has acted as a major conditioning factor on European trends in the direction of unity. There is apparently a deeply seated conviction that integration would serve the American interest as well as that of Europe and a peaceful prosperous world at large. It was perhaps in this spirit that the Fulbright resolution of March 1947, recording in lapidary language that "Congress favors the creation of a United States of Europe," was passed through both houses of Congress. The economic side of the American case for integration appears very forcefully in the preamble of the Foreign Assistance Act of April 1948: "Mindful of the advantages which the United States has enjoyed through the existence of a large domestic market with no internal trade barriers, and believing that similar advantages can accrue to the countries of Europe, it is declared to be the policy of the people of the United States to encourage these countries through a joint organization to exert sustained common efforts . . . which will speedily achieve that economic cooperation in Europe which is essential for lasting peace and prosperity." Thus Mr. Paul Hoffman was taking up a familiar theme when he told the Council of OEEC in October 1949 that "the people and the Congress of the United States" (and, as he hoped, a great majority of Europeans) "have instinctively felt that economic integration is essential if there is to be an end to Europe's recurring economic crises." The policy implications of what earlier had been a rather vague conception became clearer.

However, the emphasis placed on integration since mid-1947 has been due to more concrete and urgent motives than an instinctive desire to see Western Europe shaped in the image of the United States. It is related to the profound readjustment of United States political and economic foreign policy enforced by the deflation of its hopes for peace based on voluntary collaboration between the Soviet Union and the first-ranking powers. The "Truman Doctrine," the Soviet rejection of the Marshall offer and their formation of "Cominform" and "Comecon" (the Soviet equivalent of ECA [Economic Cooperation Administraton]), the Czechoslovak coup, and the deadlock of the Big Four foreign ministers' council dampened hopes for great-power cooperation in bringing a stable, prosperous and peaceful Europe into being.

It has long been obvious that American championship of the concept of European integration has been matched by violent hostility to this idea on the part of the Soviet Union. In fact, Soviet opposition to any regional 'bloc' in Western Europe long antedates the present East-West conflict. The Soviet Union condemned Briand's "European Union" and other prewar proposals, and in 1943 voiced its disapproval of tentative discussions among European governments-in-exile in London concerning the study of customs union projects after the war.

As Western Europe constituted after North America the most important regional component of that "free world" which United States policy now set out to secure, it was but logical for it to stress to Europe the theme that strength lay in unity. Since economic viability, ideological cohesion, morale and military strength are all essential factors in "total defense," it was also logical to advance on all these planes—political, military, economic—the plea that the strength and prosperity of an "integrated" Europe would be greater than the sum of its separate national units. These considerations introduced the "integration" theme into that movement of United States security policy away from "globalism" and towards "regionalism" which culminated in the North Atlantic Treaty. However, American policy has not been clear on the precise place of an "integrated" Western European region in this thinking. The ultimate aim, perhaps, is a Western Europe—somehow defined—which is both economically "viable" and capable of self-defense out of its own resources. For the foreseeable future, however, the North Atlantic pact gives substance to the concept of an "Atlantic community" in which two North American nations join hands with ten European states. Is the concept one of North American cooperation with Western

Europe, combined with integration in Western Europe? Or is it one of "Atlantic integration"? These and similar questions are for the future. Not all cooperative action need be based on the use of new international organizations. Thus the United States has occasionally tackled some common problems through a "key nations" or "oligarchic" approach (e.g. the Anglo-Canadian-United States talks before British devaluation or the International Materials Conference "steered" by the United States, Britain and France).

Much of the emphasis in American policy has been on economic integration, perhaps because the furnishing of aid to Europe provided the United States with a lever to move Europe into joint action on economic matters. In this sphere, too, a swing from "globalism" to "regionalism" has occurred in American foreign economic policy, again resulting in somewhat confusing paradoxes.

Western European economic integration was not among the early postwar objectives of American foreign economic policy. On the contrary, it would have conflicted with the commitment to a world-wide multilateral economic system governed by the principles of nondiscrimination. Such a system was the aim of United States sponsorship of schemes like the International Monetary Fund or the International Trade Organization. In its draft charters for the latter, the United States adhered to the traditional position that any preferential arrangements among sovereign states short of a full customs union were inconsistent with the most-favored-nation obligation by which nondiscrimination was to be mainly enforced.

It was not until mid-1947 . . . that preference for European economic integration was expressed by American policy. It was injected, rather vaguely at first, when Secretary of State Marshall stipulated the condition of cooperative European "self-help" as a prerequisite to American aid. Increasing emphasis has been put on this preference since late 1949, when it crystallized into a desire to see Western Europe welded into a "single market."

This endorsement of economic regionalism in Europe, however, was not accompanied by any clarification as to how it was to be reconciled with the earlier, and continued, commitment to nondiscriminatory "globalism." One result has been the emergence of two parallel sets of international economic arrangements involving most Western European nations. There are the older "global" schemes like International Monetary Fund and the General Agreement on Tariffs and Trade (GATT) (conceived as forerunner of International Trade Organization and now probably destined to be its substitute), which would help to integrate Western European nations, separately, with the world economy (and thus incidentally reduce the economic significance of political frontiers in Europe). There are also the more recent schemes, like the European Payments Union, the OEEC trade liberalization agreements, and the Schuman Plan which regard Western Europe (or parts of it) as an "economic region" and strive to reduce barriers within the area without reducing barriers around it. Possibilities of conflict inherent in this parallelism may be illustrated by the Schuman Plan: if its participants abolish barriers to trade among themselves, they would be required, as parties to the General Agreement on Tariffs and Trade to admit the coal and steel of nonmembers also free of duties and other restrictions (unless GATT signatories agree, by a two-thirds majority to waive the most-favored-nation privileges).

Uncertainty as to how the United States proposed to reconcile this conflict tended to guide early European response to the integration plea into directions which, while possibly steering clear of the problem described above, were also those which proved most difficult to put into effect. . . . What growing realization there has been of the advantages of unity has been prompted mainly by the Soviet-Communist menace—a powerful but, one hopes, temporary challenge to stand together. If this compulsion were removed one would see much less "integration" activity than goes on today. Similarly, one would see less of it but for the American backing given to the "integration" ideal as a "string" attached to United States aid. . . . As seen by probably a majority of Europeans, current formulas for political integration fail to solve the problem of how to unite and yet preserve that diversity—including national diversity—which with all its drawbacks is also a positive feature of the "European way of life," and in any case one that would be exceedingly hard to eradicate.

A number of factors in Europe which impede progress towards economic integration must also be kept in mind. Before the Far Eastern crisis radically rearranged priorities for Western Europe, movement towards the ideal of a single market had been initiated primarily in response to American prodding. An impressive measure of cooperation on urgent tasks had been achieved, but most attempts to extend such *ad hoc* efforts had run into difficult problems soon after their inception. Identification of these stumbling blocks to further progress has been valuable in itself. It helps to measure the gap between what the United States has postulated as desirable and what is attainable; and also it helps to appraise what Europeans will and will not accept as desirable. Superficial impressions that Western Europe has been guilty of inexcusable inertia and inaction should be qualified in the light of at least the following considerations.

The impact of the lack of integration on Europe's economy should not be exaggerated. Receiving important but diminishing American aid, Western Europe in 1945-1950 performed a feat of economic recovery which compares very favorably with that after World War I, although the starting point was far less propitious. Productivity in European industry has risen, and in most countries continues to rise, at rates much higher than prewar. Intra-European trade (a significant measure of "integration") increased in volume from 70 per cent of the 1938 level in early 1948 to 145 per cent late in 1950.

Progress towards the "single market" is opposed by pressures upon national governments from vested interests of business, farmers, and labor. Such pressures, however detrimental to productivity, are exceedingly difficult to remove in a democratic framework. In fact, in Europe as in the United States, their interplay makes up the substance of democracy. It is easier to condemn, say, the opposition of French farmers to tariff reductions than it is to show how any French government could ride roughshod over the preferences of its farm bloc and stay in office.

The power of private monopolies and their activities in restraint of competition is also more easily condemned than abolished. No European country has anti-trust legislation even as moderately effective as that of the United States, although several have cautiously moved in that direction. Moreover, European business has traditionally regarded cartels and similar arrangements as a highly desirable form of market organization. . . .

Most European governments have faced, since the war, the difficult policy problem of combating postwar inflation while at the same time avoiding heavy unemployment which the need for social cohesion and political stability made unacceptable. This also discouraged experiments in integration which, regardless of beneficial long-range effects, threatened dislocation and reduced employment or incomes in the short run.

Regional economic integration is in many respects too "parochial" a solution to the problems of a region as closely interwoven with the world economy as the "workshop" of Europe. For several countries which depend particularly on overseas economic ties, and/or have colonial or other political affiliations outside Europe, this problem becomes an important conditioning factor in their attitude to integration. . . .

While the integration issue has generally evoked more apathy than controversy in Europe, an exception is provided by the steady exchange of recriminations between the Continent and Britain (also the United States and Britain) over that attitude which in this country has been widely labeled as "Britain dragging its feet." Some landmarks in the record which earned this reputation for Britain were set by its rejection of France's European Assembly and Customs Union proposals in June 1948; subsequent efforts to withhold any genuine authority from the Council of Europe; British stalling on the European Payments Union plan; the refusal to join the Schuman scheme; and the rigidly insular Labor Party foreign policy platform of June 1950. . . .

The British Government has pleaded in its defense that it is second to none in its desire to see a united Europe, but that it (a) has views of its own as to how this goal should be pursued; (b) has empire and other responsibilities outside Europe which put it in a "special position"; (c) . . . has done as much [as] or more than any European nation on behalf of integration, while talking less about it than some. . . . They also find membership in a European federation hard or impossible to reconcile with Britain's place in the political structure of the Commonwealth. They prefer a "functional" approach to integration, through intergovernmental cooperation . . . as exemplified by OEEC or NATO . . . avoiding ventures into untried and controversial supranational authorities. . . . The concept of an Atlantic community is more likely to win active British support than that of a European union. "Functional" cooperation in defense and economic matters on an Atlantic scale would go far to meet British misgivings. . . . Whether Britain will also be willing to shed its suspicions of federation if it were offered on an Atlantic scale (as recently proposed by Senator Gillette and others) would probably largely depend on United States (and Canadian) willingness to join such a scheme. . . .

The challenge offered by the need for the rehabilitation of war devastated Europe and by the dollar gap problem resulted in the creation of organizations initially conceived as . . . temporary agencies. The habits and procedures of intergovernmental cooperation developed in these agencies may well result in more permanent cooperative effort. . . . Acceptance of the principles of "balanced collective forces" makes it doubtful whether a return to the old system of national defense is possible.

MEANING OF EUROPEAN UNION [2]

When our own United States was formed, it contained less than four million people. Today, by contrast, the nations of France, Italy, Western Germany, the Netherlands, Belgium and Luxembourg include some 160 million people. The governments of these countries have embarked upon a course of action which is aimed at the political and economic union of their respective countries.

An act of political creation of profound historical importance is now occurring in Western Europe.

Today many Americans are asking three questions: "What is meant by European union?" "Why should we care about European union?" "What, if anything, should we do about it?"

[2] From "The United States of Europe," by Beardsley Ruml, fiscal expert, writer and educator. *Collier's.* 129:22+. June 21, 1952. Reprinted by permission.

European union is not a new postwar idea. It has been a living and a growing movement for many centuries. A suggestion for a voluntary United States of Europe was approved by Henry IV, King of France, in 1638. A century and a half later, the German philosopher, Immanuel Kant, discussed a similar idea. And in 1929 a Premier of France, Aristide Briand, proposed a European union on behalf of his government.

In its long history, Europe has experienced other unification movements of a very different character. These were the short-lived empires of Napoleon Bonaparte and Adolf Hitler, built by conquest and maintained by force.

Today, in contrast, the emerging union of the Western European nations is a voluntary one based on mutual respect, consent, and recognition that unification is necessary for survival. If wisely devised and successfully protected, this new European union, the product of our own times, may be expected to have a long and fruitful development.

As long as the states of Western Europe were individually able to discharge the responsibilities of sovereignty, European union could be nothing more than a romantic ideal. But, in 1940, long-established national states fell with rapidity before the Nazi armies. After the war, an increasingly large number of thoughtful people throughout the world realized the truth of what a smaller number had been saying for many years: that the persistent weaknesses of the nations of Europe were not the transitory effects of two world wars within a generation, but were signs that many of Europe's national states could no longer live independently as economic and political units. This understanding made European union a short-time goal of practical policy.

The leading statesmen of postwar Europe vigorously espoused the cause of union. Churchill in England, Schuman and Monnet in France, Adenauer in Germany, Sforza in Italy, Spaak in Belgium gave thought and eloquence to the promotion of European union. Associations of private citizens sprang up throughout Western Europe, with membership across boundary lines, to crystallize public sentiment in its favor.

While private citizens were informing public opinion and devising concrete proposals directed toward union, public officials and government leaders were also active. Practical difficulties and practical solutions of these difficulties were explored in new intergovernmental agencies like the Organization for European Economic Cooperation, the Council of Europe, the European Payments Union, and the European Coal and Steel Community (Schuman Plan).

These international organizations in Western Europe have come into being only within the last five years and they have already built up a body of practical experience in the joint exercise of national sovereignty. They have unified Western Europe economically and politically to a degree without precedent in Europe's modern history. Already certain specific and separable economic and defense functions are being handled by "supranational" organizations, agencies which are to a greater or lesser extent above the national governments which created them.

However, the possibilities of further progress in unification in the strictly economic and defense fields seem to be coming to an end. The recent agreement, now waiting ratification by national parliaments, among the governments of France, Italy, West Germany and the Low Countries to merge their armed forces in a common European army revealed that the essential features of a unified defense establishment could be achieved only if a formal political and economic union were also in the process of being developed. For a common foreign policy, a common military budget, a central procurement agency, a united Chiefs of Staff, standardization of weapons, training and military doctrine—not to mention the requirements of loyalty, discipline and sacrifice—would be unthinkable without a full union.

And so the final agreement under which the European army is to be created pledges its six member governments to try to form such a union during a transition period of three years. Sometime before the end of that period, these countries expect to hold a constitutional convention to work out the political details of the union.

Americans, when they have thought about it at all, have taken a friendly interest in the growth of the European union movement. We are convinced that our own history has amply justified our own federation of states. And we can see no other hope that Europe's troubles can be overcome.

But beyond this friendly interest, there is recognition that the United States has a deep concern in the progress of European union. Americans want to help build an effective world order—a workable world economy in which we and others can prosper, and a world political system in which all will be secure. To this end, the restoration of Europe's economic health, political stability and capacity for self-defense is essential.

We have recognized, in a series of aid programs culminating in the Marshall Plan, the need for a rapid infusion of working capital into these countries in order to prevent the collapse of their economies. The revival of Western Europe means rising productivity, a more equitable division of income, heightened morale and confidence in the future, greater economic freedom and incentives for increased initiative and enterprise.

This revival of Western Europe's economic health, political strength and capacity for defense is a vital condition for checking decisively Soviet aggression, for maintaining world peace and for promoting world prosperity—in all of which the United States has a deep concern.

For the achievement in Western Europe of economic self-support, of effective democratic institutions and of successful measures of defense, a political and economic union is clearly indispensable, now that its separate national states have shown that they are no longer capable of attaining these goals individually. . . . And today, as the movement toward unification approaches the point of political federation, its achievements are no longer mere formal diplomatic triumphs but have come to have great significance to the average citizen.

Thus, European union will benefit not only Europe but ourselves as well. It will promote the objectives of our foreign policy—prosperity and peace. . . .

The next steps toward European union involve decisions of great complexity and difficulty. It is of the utmost importance that the right decisions be made, for the results, good or ill, will be with us for years. With rapid and decisive progress toward union, Western Europe will become a self-supporting, powerful and voluntary associate of the United States in strengthening world order and security. . . . Although a sympathetic partner, a united Europe will not and should not be a mere satellite of the United States.

This year and the next will mark a turning point both for the Europeans and for ourselves. . . .

The economic and political ties which link the six union-minded Western European nations to one another are already far stronger than those which [once] existed among the thirteen American colonies. The common cultural heritage of these European countries is obvious. And they too are hastening their unification under the impulse of a common crisis.

The agreement by the six nations to establish a unified European army contains some remarkable parallels to our early American experience. During the three-year transition period, until the stage of formal union is reached, the individual national governments will continue to raise and to equip their own troops for assignment to the central command. They will make available to the central headquarters only such funds as the member governments decide that it should have. Just as in the American government under the Articles of Confederation, the new central organs in Europe will not possess the tax power or the police power.

But these transitional arrangements must be recognized for what they are. With us, the colonial leaders came to recognize that neither political stability, nor economic progress, nor even adequate military defense could be secured without a stronger central government. Accordingly, the Articles of Confederation were replaced in 1789 by our present Constitution and a true federal union was thereby established.

The logic of this development is apparent to the leaders of the European movement and, as we have seen, they have made provision in the European Army Agreement for the calling of a constitutional convention at an early date as the next step toward a fuller political union. . . .

One can look in vain for monster petitions, mass demonstrations, enormous parades and other melodramatic devices whereby popular enthusiasm is aroused and made manifest. Nevertheless, recent tests of public opinion indicate that only a small percentage of the people of France, Italy, Western Germany and the Low Countries are opposed to European union.

European union is being built by a relatively small group of farsighted statesmen and thinkers who understand the need and who are also sensitive to the measure of popular support on which they can depend. . . .

In spite of all this, great difficulties remain to be overcome. The nations of Western Europe are industrialized countries with highly complex economies. In each of these countries there are powerful interests which have come to rely upon preferential economic policies of their national governments, including the protection afforded by tariffs and other barriers to trade.

Only with the establishment of a broad continental market will the low costs and high living standards of mass-production industry be realized for the welfare of the people of Western Europe.

Unification on a broad enough scale will make the task of abolishing tariffs and other protective barriers easier. For example, Belgium and the Netherlands both specialize in the production and export of certain fresh fruits and vegetables. A union consisting, in effect, of only these two countries, like the abortive "Benelux" (Belgium-Netherlands-Luxembourg) union of the immediate postwar years, is bound to encounter great difficulties because the agricultural products of the two countries are competitive.

But once other European countries are included in the union, a wider market is provided for the fruits and vegetables of both Belgium and the Netherlands. The farmers of neither country need worry unduly about those of the other, and their mutual competition for the European market can have healthy results in lower prices and greater productivity.

There will nevertheless remain a number of industries which, in the short run, can be hurt by the competition of more efficient producers in other parts of the union. These will probably need some sort of readjustment assistance in modernizing their equipment, retraining their workers or moving their plants to more economic locations. Belgian coal mines cannot now compete with those of the Ruhr; many Italian steel plants are uneconomic by German or even French standards; German luxury goods are not nearly so desirable as French or Italian. But, over the longer run, the readjustments which will take place owing to the dropping of trade and exchange barriers among the members will make the union's industry far more efficient than it was originally.

The task of unification will involve also the harmonizing of disparate national economic conditions. Prices; tax and subsidy rates; wage and employment levels, and banking, fiscal and monetary practices will have to be made consistent. Uniform legal codes, particularly as they affect business, will be needed. It will take a considerable period of time before these necessary adjustments can be made and there is general freedom of movement for persons, goods and capital within the union. But, fortunately, these necessary adjustments do not need to be made all at once.

Then, too, there are language differences, divergences in political forms and traditions, and variances of religious belief and expression.

These Western European countries were for a long time powerful and independent national states, and their former period of national greatness and of traditional national enmities is still too recent to be quickly forgotten.

Fortunately, the notion of Europe as a political entity has never disappeared from the minds of its people because of the rise of separate nationalisms, and since World War II, there has been a remarkable revival of the concept of "the European" as disinct from "the Frenchman," "the German" and so forth. . . .

Some Americans and Europeans have been disturbed by the unwillingness of Britain and the Scandinavian countries to join the emerging European union. It would probably be a better union if they did, but their absence will not be a fatal shortcoming.

Moreover, an attempt to include them in the union at this time would immeasurably increase the practical difficulties of unification and would slow down the process to the point where much of the present momentum would be lost.

Nor do the British need union with the Continent for the solution of their own problems. Despite its very grave economic difficulties, Britain is still a "going concern" as a national state. It already enjoys, in the globe-encircling Commonwealth and sterling area, membership in a large economic and political unit. Some of these advantages would have to be sacrificed if Britain were to become a full member of a European union.

However, there would be marked benefits both for Britain and for the Continent if some form of special economic relationship—short of full membership—could be worked out between Britain and the Continental union. Similarly, the solution of Britain's persistent balance-of-payments problem may sooner or later require some sort of special economic relationship between Britain and the United States. Thus, Britain might in time become a binding link between the two larger members of the North Atlantic community—the United States and United Europe.

The unification of Europe is historically inevitable. The only questions are how soon it will occur and what kind of union it will be. In the past 150 years, Western Europe has been twice unified by force, under the short-lived empires of Napoleon and Hitler. . . . But the only kind of union that has a chance of lasting and of progressing to better forms of social order is one based on voluntary consent. This is the only kind of union with which we and the other free peoples of the world can live in security and in mutual cooperation.

European unification on a voluntary basis will also provide practical lessons in how to bring about larger developments. It will give hope that over the long years the process of political consolidation can occur on an even wider scale.

Finally we come to this question: What, if anything, should we do about it? Should we be mere spectators of the development of European union, or is there a more active and helpful role which we should be playing in this historic process? Obviously we are concerned in the success of the unification movement on a voluntary basis. If, then, our help can be given usefully, we should be prepared to play our proper part.

In the progress toward union already made by Europeans . . .
our influence has been a catalytic agent which has speeded up
reactions without losing its own identity. Our economic aid has
been decisive in the establishment and successful operation of
new central institutions like the Organization for European
Economic Cooperation and the European Payments Union, since
it provided them with resources separate from those supplied by
their member governments. It is owing to the existence of these
funds that, in many instances, the decisions and programs of
these international agencies have won the acceptance of national
governments.

The United States has also provided encouragement to European leadership. The rate of progress has been accelerated by
the knowledge in Europe that many Americans believed European union to be necessary, by the prestige of American individuals who actively spoke out for it, and by the fact that the
Congress of the United States has declared that the encouragement of European unification is a major objective of our foreign
aid. . . .

What forms should our help to the unification movement
take? Obviously, it would be neither appropriate nor effective
for the United States to make the achievement of European
union an absolute condition for the extension of our economic
and military aid. Such an attempt on our part would do more
harm than good. The threat to cut off our aid unless the Europeans united would not produce a voluntary European union and
would be the action of a bully, not that of a friend.

Our role in the future should be like that of the past. We
must make unmistakably clear at all times our support of the
objective of a European union. We must express our expectation
that progress will be made toward union by the Europeans themselves. We must be 'willing, as in the past, to assist the new
central economic institutions with financial support, and we
must express our preference for extending economic and military
aid to Western Europe through such central institutions as they
come into being.

Outside the area of the six Western European countries,
other developments are necessary to ensure the early success of

their union. Failure to solve the problem of Britain's economic future and the consequent recurring sterling crises would have a most unsettling effect on a developing European union, even though Britain is not a member of it. Also, our own domestic and foreign trade policies must be made more consistent with Europe's need to earn more dollars—and Europe must earn more dollars if it is ever to become self-supporting in any real sense. The United States, in becoming better integrated into the world economy, will at the same time assist the unification of Western Europe.

THE COUNCIL OF EUROPE [3]

The Statute of London of May 5, 1949 . . . created the Council of Europe. . . . It has been an outgrowth of the Brussels Treaty of March 17, 1948, and of the Benelux experience. But in the larger sense the Council of Europe and its most conspicuous agency, the Strasbourg Assembly, reach back through the ages and are connected historically with the Concert of Europe, the Napoleonic confederations, the Holy Roman Empire, the medieval concept of a united Christendom, and the Roman imperium.

The Council of Europe represents an attempt to solve many of Europe's urgent contemporary problems. . . . The Council . . . provides the peoples of Western Europe with a framework within which they may integrate national economies—communications, transportation, currencies, production, and social security—across national barriers and thereby overcome and compensate for some of the unfavorable and destructive forces which in recent years have all but wrecked their economies. It also represents an attempt to combat communism both from within and from without. Moreover, it holds out hope of solving the German problem by fitting Germany into the larger economic and political life of Europe. . . . Finally, the Council of Europe is an effort to render Europe a "third force" in the world, to make her again economically productive and politically powerful, to give her the weight to which her resources and technology and the intelligence of her people entitle her. . . .

[3] From "What of the Council of Europe?" by William G. Carleton, Professor of Political Science, University of Florida. *Virginia Quarterly Review.* 27:179-95. Spring 1951. Reprinted by permission.

The Council is composed of fifteen nations. Ten of these were original members: Britain, France, Italy, Belgium, the Netherlands, Sweden, Norway, Denmark, the Irish Republic, and Luxembourg. Five have been added since May of 1949: Turkey, Greece, Iceland, Germany, and the Saar.

The aim of the Council, as set forth in Article One of the Statute of London, is "to achieve a greater unity between its members for the purpose of safeguarding and realizing the ideals and principles which are their common heritage and facilitating their economic and social progress." This aim is to be pursued "through the organs of the Council by discussion of questions of common concern and by agreements and common action in economic, social, cultural, scientific, legal, and administrative matters and in the maintenance and further realization of human rights and fundamental freedoms." This statement of purpose is, of course, vague and will mean much or little depending upon future developments. Matters of defense are specifically excluded from the competence of the Council under Article One.

The Council of Europe has three main organs: the Committee of Ministers, the Consultative Assembly, and the Secretariat. The foreign minister of each member-state becomes *ex officio* his nation's representative on the Committee of Ministers. The Consultative Assembly consists of representatives of each member-state appointed in such manner as the government of that member-state shall determine. Member-states are equal in the Committee of Ministers, where each has one vote, but in the Assembly representation is based largely on population. Britain, France, Italy, and the German Federal Republic have each the same number of representatives in the Assembly, and each has far more representatives than are allotted any other member. Luxembourg, Iceland, and the Saar have the smallest number of representatives. The total number of representatives in the Assembly actually present and recorded on roll calls usually runs somewhat around one hundred. The chiefs of the Secretariat are appointed by the Consultative Assembly on the recommendation of the Committee of Ministers.

Since the adoption of the Statute of London two additional agencies of importance have evolved, revealing the organic nature of a developing political entity. One is the Standing Committee (or the Permanent Commission) of the Assembly. This is a sort of "Little Assembly," consisting of twenty-three members, which meets at regular intervals between sessions of the Assembly and insures continuity. The other is the Joint Committee consisting of four members of the Committee of Ministers and five members of the Standing Committee of the Assembly. The function of the Joint Committee is to act as a liaison between the Committee of Ministers and the Assembly. The Assembly meets at Strasbourg once a year, and the Secretariat has its permanent seat in that city. The Committee of Ministers, the Standing Committee, and the Joint Committee usually meet at the Quai d'Orsay in Paris.

For the most part, the Statute of London contemplates that the initiative for constructive action is the responsibility of the Committee of Ministers. It is the Committee of Ministers which is enjoined to further the aims of the Council of Europe by undertaking conventions and agreements and by recommending action by the governments of the member-states. The Consultative Assembly can discuss only those matters which have been referred to it by the Committee of Ministers or which have been approved by the Committee for inclusion in the agenda of the Assembly. In making recommendations to governments, the vote of the Committee of Ministers must be unanimous. This veto power of the Committee of Ministers, which in effect is a veto by any one of the member-states, has become a stumbling block to the development of effective powers in the Council of Europe. In referring matters for discussion to the Assembly and in approving the Assembly agenda, the vote in the Committee of Ministers is by a two-thirds majority of the representatives casting a vote, and of a majority of the representatives entitled to sit in the Committee, but even here, when the question is deemed of "importance," the Committee by resolution passed by a two-thirds majority may require the vote to be unanimous.

In spite of its agenda having to be approved by the Committee of Ministers, the Assembly in fact enjoys a wide latitude of debate. Indeed, the Committee of Ministers has laid it down that in practice it would not exercise its right of control to fix the agenda for the Assembly's meeting "so long as the subjects placed on the agenda fall within the scope of the Council of Europe as defined by the Statute."

The chief and most important conflict in . . . [the 1951] Assembly . . . was over the extent and the form of a politically unified Europe. Some of the delegates favored limiting unification to the inter-governmental approach; some favored extending it to actual federalism—federalism *now;* some favored a functional approach such as the Schuman Plan and other economic and social authorities, with the feeling that out of a functional approach ultimately would come a federal state.

In general, the British and Scandinavian delegates favored limiting cooperation to the inter-governmental approach as illustrated by the European Payments Union created by the OEEC [Organization for European Economic Cooperation]. There, it was argued, was an example of an effective operation of inter-governmental experts, always subject to the control of the national governments. Speaking for the inter-governmentalists, Hugh Dalton said in effect that the British and Scandinavian peoples did not want federation. Any insistence upon federalism within the Council of Europe would, he said, wreck it. . . . And why is federalism less popular in Britain and Scandinavia than in other parts of Western Europe? In part, the opposition springs from the relatively higher standard of living in Britain and Scandinavia and the fear that federation would jeopardize it. In part, the opposition springs from political considerations— many Scandinavians still hope to stay out of the political differences of the rest of Europe and many Britons, thinking in the older terms, fear that a federal Europe would prove too powerful a makeweight to Britain in Europe and would be inconsistent with Britain's agreements with the non-European states of the British Commonwealth. Moreover, Britain and Scandinavia have far less to fear from Communist penetration from within.

At the opposite extreme were the federalists, those who favored turning the Council of Europe into a federal state, and doing it at once. . . . Federalism was strongest in the Italian and French delegations because of desperate economic conditions in Italy, defeatism and unrest of the working classes in France, and fear of the Italian and French Communists. The federalists bitterly resented the attitudes of the inter-governmentalists. They pointed to observers from the British dominions present at Strasbourg and declared there was no irreconcilable inconsistency between British commitments as a European power and as a member of the Commonwealth. They maintained that the one achievement of inter-governmentalism—the OEEC—had been disappointing. They charged that Britain, instead of taking the lead in making European currencies convertible, had become a member of the Payments Union only under American pressure; that Britain had dodged her share in dismantling the barriers to inter-European trade by insisting that the liberalization agreement should exclude all imports on government account. These imports into Socialist Britain are both large in volume and of the kind the Continent can supply. Such behavior, it was said, causes irritation and accounts for the brusque manner in which the Schuman Plan was launched and explains why it has become the test case of the functional approach. But, it was argued, even had the OEEC been successful, it did not go far enough or touch enough areas of cooperation. The federalists also pointed to the delays in the Schuman Plan because of the opposition of the inter-governmentalists.

The federalists insisted that they had come to Strasbourg to create a federal state, if not directly, then indirectly by extending the functional approach of the Schuman Plan to more and more areas. They proclaimed that they were for federalism, or functionalism that led to federalism, and that they were willing to go ahead at once with or without the inter-governmentalists, with or without Britain and Scandinavia. . . . In the end the federalists were defeated by the firm stand of Guy Mollet and the behind-the-scenes activity of Spaak. . . . The defeat of the federalists opened the way for a compromise—the more leisurely functional approach.

This third approach, the one designated by its chief sponsors, Schuman and Jean Monnet, as "the functional-federal" approach, is chiefly represented by the Schuman Plan. . . .

Whether or not Europe goes ahead with federation, some of the practices of the Strasbourg Assembly may well prove valuable for future usage in international organization. Particularly is this true of the way in which national delegations are selected, their large latitude of individual responsibility, their freedom from national government control—all of which is in striking contrast to the way national delegations in the old League of Nations and in the present-day United Nations have operated. In the United Nations, national delegations are chosen by the executive power and speak for that power. The delegates from a given nation sit together, they vote and act officially *en bloc*. Every national delegation presents a solid front *vis à vis* every other national delegation. National solidarity is never broken; the nations appear to have no political divisions within. All of this tends to make international bodies merely additional arenas for the playing of nationalistic balance-of-power politics.

In the Strasbourg Assembly the practice is quite different. True, the delegations usually are chosen by the executives of their respective national governments. But the custom has grown up of appointing delegations representing the different and conflicting political opinions existing inside the countries themselves. . . .

The result of these arrangements is that national delegations split; political groups in one country make alliances with similar groups in other countries and against dissimilar groups in their own country. The process of group conflict and compromise, characteristic of national domestic politics, bursts national boundaries and extends itself to international politics. Thus the illusion of national political solidarity is shattered, and people tend to think in group terms over a wider international area. This is the way to true federalism, to the building of a truly international society. . . .

The practice in the Strasbourg Assembly of national delegations representing different classes, groups, and parties *inside* their countries is the most important contribution to internationalism made by the Council of Europe. Indeed, this may well be the most important contribution to internationalism made by any international body to the present time. Even should a genuine federal state in Western Europe fail to materialize, this is a practice which might well be carried over to other international bodies. As a matter of fact, the degree to which the party and group conflict of domestic politics is carried over into international politics is perhaps the most valid test of whether internationalism, as distinguished from nationalism, is really emerging.

CONGRESSIONAL VIEW OF EUROPEAN UNITY [4]

[On May 12, 1951, the Consultative Assembly of the Council of Europe asked delegations from the United States Congress to meet a similar delegation from the Consultative Assembly to discuss "problems of common interest." Congress approved the meeting, October 18, 1951, appointing seven senators and seven representatives to the delegation— the first occasion that an official delegation from the United States Congress has participated in discussions of this kind with representatives of an organization like the Council of Europe. The meeting was held at Strasbourg prior to the regular meeting of the Consultative Assembly, and lasted five days, November 19-23, 1951. It was strictly unofficial, involving no commitment on the part of either group. The European delegation comprised eighteen members from twelve nations—all bona fide representatives to the Consultative Assembly. The following are excerpts from the report of the congressional delegation—Ed.]

The American delegation was deeply impressed with the view that both economic and political union of some character is vital to the defense of the Western Hemisphere countries. . . .

The Congress has repeatedly, in its bills for European aid, made it clear that one of the main purposes of the tremendous appropriations that it has made was to aid in unification of the Western European countries. . . .

It is the general aim of the United States in providing assistance to Western Europe to help free Europe to build her economic

[4] From "The Union of Europe," report of the meetings between a delegation appointed by Congress and representatives appointed by the Consultative Assembly of the Council of Europe, November 1951, presented by Senator Theodore Francis Green, chairman of the Senate delegation. (Senate Document no90) 82d Congress, 2d session. Superintendent of Documents. Washington, D.C. January 21, 1952. p5-19.

and defensive military strength as rapidly as possible so that free Europe can defend itself from internal and external threats of aggression. European self-sufficiency in these regards is essential to the security of the United States. In efforts to achieve this end the Congress provided in the Mutual Security Act of 1951 that assistance is furnished in order to further "encourage the economic and the political federation of Europe. . . ."

Within this general framework, the joint committee of the Congress which attended meetings with representatives of the Consultative Assembly of the Council of Europe, unanimously reports these conclusions:

1. There is general confusion among the nations and peoples of Western Europe as to the respective roles of the Council of Europe, the NATO, and the proposed Atlantic Union, particularly with regard to the part each should play in building economic and defensive military strength in free Europe. To some extent this confusion may be attributable to lack of clarity as to the policies of both the United States and Great Britain.

2. Members of the Consultative Assembly of the Council of Europe are not agreed as to whether that organization should take immediate steps resulting in some degree of federation or proceed toward that ultimate goal on a project by project basis.

3. While it seems clear that as of the present time the United Kingdom does not expect to participate fully in any truly political federation which may be developed in Western Europe, there is considerable doubt also as to the nature and extent of British participation in organizations that may be established to deal with such specific suggestions as the Pleven plan, the Schuman Plan, and the proposals for a European agricultural market.

4. Regardless of the attitude of the United Kingdom and certain countries, the American delegation felt that those Western European countries willing to move closer toward economic and political federation should do so as rapidly as possible.

5. The failure of Western Europe to make more realistic progress toward European unification results in large part, in the opinion of the delegation, from a tendency to overemphasize the

difficulties of unification and to underestimate the dangers that will inevitably flow from failure to unify.

6. While economic and military assistance for Western Europe is provided because a majority in Congress believe that it is in the best interests of the United States to provide such aid, it does not follow that assistance must be given without attaching conditions to that aid. Thus far Congress has not sought to make its aid conditional upon the achievement of some specific degree of economic or political federation in Western Europe. Whether such conditions should be attached is a matter upon which the delegation does not express a conclusion; it notes for the record, however, that past legislative references to economic and political integration have not brought forth the positive achievements which many members of Congress expected to flow from such references and other means may need to be chosen to achieve those results.

FUNCTIONAL APPROACH TO INTEGRATION [5]

New phenomena in Europe are labeled by new words. "Integration" is one of them. The expression "functional approach" is another. Europe's plight does indeed call for an entirely new approach and for the application of drastic remedies. . . .

Unification must be carefully planned, and carried out step by step, for a premature move would actually encourage the disruptive tendencies. The program cannot be constructed by analogy from antiquity or the Middle Ages, nor even from the impressive example of the United States. It must fit the particular circumstances of the Continent. Eastern Europe has been integrated forcibly, at the expense of democracy and independence. Western Europe strives for the voluntary cooperation of free peoples, without the destruction of those qualities or of their healthy variety. The form of organization must help meet immediate needs, but must be one from which a European federation can develop.

[5] From "The Functional Approach to European Integration," by Dirk U. Stikker, Minister of Foreign Affairs of the Netherlands and chairman of the Organization for European Economic Cooperation. *Foreign Affairs.* 29:436-44. April 1951. Reprinted by permission.

There is no single center of European gravity around which the nations can group to speed up this process. That is the reason why the functional approach offers the most direct path to the goal. "Functional integration" is based on the existence of very real national interests, and at the same time recognizes the necessity of subordinating separate interests more and more to the common welfare. It is based on a mixture of realism and idealism. It seeks to restrict national sovereignty, but does not attempt the feat of abolishing it at a stroke; to await the ideal situation in which complete federation becomes possible would mean never starting at all. It proposes that the countries of Western Europe at once proceed to cooperate wherever they can. Whenever a nation enters a new field of cooperation national sovereignty is transferred to a certain extent by that very fact. These new organizations create what might be called a limited federation—limited not geographically but functionally. In short, this approach does not claim to provide the final answer to Europe's problems but simply a series of practical steps forward. It is not a theoretical answer but an outcome of the concrete developments of the last few years.

A European "opinion" has crystallized in the Council of Europe. At Strasbourg the representatives of various countries are not seated according to nationalities, but in the alphabetical order of their names. In the Council, views of speakers are European rather than national. But though the Council is a symbol of desire for a greater European unity, as expressed particularly by its great champions, Mr. Churchill and Mr. Spaak, it has not been able to do much. The proponents of federation have met with opposition from the British and Scandinavian governments. The suggestion for a geographically limited federation—a "little Europe" which would omit Britain and Scandinavia—has also failed to win strong backing. The functional approach to European integration has, however, met with general approval. There is a general understanding of Britain's view that her relations with the rest of the Commonwealth are too important to be risked in experiments in Europe, and that she must search for a form of organization which does justice both to her position in Europe and that within the Commonwealth. And there is hope that organs set up to meet limited concrete needs will help solve this problem for her and for the Scandinavian countries. No one wants a "rump Europe."

Of particular projects which have been launched the Schuman Plan is the most daring and far-reaching. It involves the partial transfer of sovereignty in the crucial field of coal and steel to a supranational authority. The effort toward integration would extend to subsidiary industries. The political importance of the proposal is also great, since it offers a means of ameliorating Franco-German antagonisms and bringing Germany into partnership in the European community.

In the summer of 1950 several other proposals inspired by the desire for European unity were submitted to the OEEC. The suggestion made by the writer—the so-called Stikker plan—is thoroughly functional. It aims to promote integration in various lines of industry not only by abolishing quantitative import restrictions but also by reducing the high tariffs which, if left at their present levels, will make the removal of quantitative restrictions an empty gesture. Indeed, their present partial removal is harmful to the smaller countries with a tradition of free trade and low tariffs, notably the Benelux nations, for it permits imports from abroad to come in easily while high tariffs elsewhere prevent these countries from finding a market for their exports.

The plan is also intended to help solve the problem of marginal industries. A real integration which facilitates a more rational organization of industry will inevitably result in considerable difficulties. The writer believes this difficulty should be met by the establishment of a European integration fund, which would have as its object the creation of new opportunities of employment. The coordination of internal monetary and fiscal policies of the various countries, to avoid inflationary or deflationary tendencies which endanger full employment, would also be sought.

The so-called Mansholt plan, submitted by the Netherlands Minister of Agriculture, broadens these ideas to cover the special difficulties of European agriculture. It starts with the realistic acknowledgment that the creation at short notice of a single European market for agriculture is impossible. Agricultural products are of vital strategic importance. No European country can permit even its least remunerative agricultural soil to be unused. Moveover, farmers perform essential social as well as economic functions; changes in the pattern of agriculture are difficult, and cannot be made overnight. Full integration will some day have to be achieved in European agriculture no less than in industry, but for the present the objective is a gradual adjustment of prices and costs in the various national markets. The plan proposes that a "European price" be fixed for various products for the participating countries. The quantity of national agricultural production will thus be determined by competition. In the course of time the price will be gradually lowered and adapted to the cost level of the most rational production method. A European integration fund will be established, in part from duties on imports from non-European nations which, as a result of "social dumping," are priced far below European costs. This fund will assist in enforcing gradual rationalization.

M. Petsche, former Minister of Economic and Financial Affairs of France, has suggested the creation of a European investment bank. This is not intended to meet the problems of the rationalization of particular lines of industry, but, generally speaking, to coordinate the investment activities of Europe along European lines. For that purpose it would if possible utilize European as well as American private capital. It might be called a first step toward an integration of investments.

The functional approach also has a part to play in the complicated field of culture. . . . The European Cultural Center and the College of Europe, both established by the International Cultural Section of the European Movement, are examples of what can be done in this field. . . .

Joint efforts for defense will strengthen these various bonds. Indeed, they already have called forth proposals for special forms of organization like the European army envisaged by M. Pleven. The first attempt at military cooperation by the five European countries which signed the Brussels Treaty was too limited to be effective. The North Atlantic Treaty made the defense of Europe a transatlantic undertaking, and brought Canada and the United States into the joint effort. European nations such as Switzerland, Sweden, Austria . . . while cooperating in the economic field through the OEEC, are not members of a European military alliance; indeed, some of them steadfastly keep aloof from it. Germany, however, has a vital role to play. No scheme of European defense can be fully effective unless Germany, the "Heartland" of the Continent, is brought in.

In military problems the functional approach is of paramount importance. The armed forces of the various nations are still "balanced" national units, designed to protect special national interests. At present the joint forces for European defense are simply the sum of these forces, with wide differences in training, equipment and organization. There must be a balanced international force, which can be operated as one unit under a single commander and in which the various national components will concentrate on those tasks for which each individual nation is best fitted. A modern army is a highly complicated affair, and only great powers can afford to produce and operate such expensive weapons as long-range bombers and heavy tanks. The functional approach would expedite recruiting and training on an international basis. For a considerable time the infantry and attached units will still be formed and trained on a national basis, though along closely coordinated lines; but international training programs could be initiated at once in special weapons such as tanks and aircraft. These would be the nucleus of a unified force. . . .

This is a joint undertaking of all the Atlantic nations. Europe, however, has a special task, for the danger to her is the most imminent and her efforts at defense have so far been inadequate. If Europe does not make a conspicuous effort of her own to match the assistance she is receiving from outside, her allies overseas will inevitably be influenced to keep their strength at home rather than risk it on Europe's battlefields. The military integration of Europe should be undertaken as a long-term program, pursued through a series of functional integrations in land, naval and air forces. Perhaps the close cooperation between Europe and the American states with the NATO may step by step create a single Atlantic community, the mainstay of a homogeneous Western civilization in which the ancient traditions of

Europe are happily blended with the dynamic vigor of the New World.

At the moment the efforts for integration in all these fields are not coordinated. Thus while the proposed High Authority for the coal and steel pool covers only some six continental countries, the power of the Atlantic Council reaches far beyond Europe. The Council of Europe might perhaps be a good center around which functional economic organs can group themselves. But it should be borne in mind that Europe is not a building which can be pulled down and rebuilt. It is a living organism which can be altered only gradually.

THE SCHUMAN PLAN [6]

Since Bismarck's time, Germany's great sources of strength have been her industrial might and her manpower. For this reason, the prospect of German foundries in full production again and German youth in uniform again arouses dread throughout Europe.

The French have brought forward two major plans designed to prevent Germany from reasserting its full might by tying the West Germans firmly to a united Western Europe. One is the Schuman Plan for pooling Western European coal and steel—the two great basic industries of war and peace. The other is the European Defense Community plan for merging national armed forces into a single European army. Last week the Schuman Plan was about ready to go into operation. It has now been ratified by all six member nations—France, Germany, Belgium, the Netherlands, Luxembourg and Italy. The Italian ratification came last Monday night.

This is how the treaty will work:

The core of Western Europe's steelmaking complex is a small triangle comprising the Lorraine iron and steel plants in France, the Saar coal mines, the Ruhr mines and mills, the Belgium mines. The greatest distance between any of these points is less than 300 miles. Compared with this, the American steel-making complex

[6] From "Schuman Treaty," news story. New York *Times.* p E2. June 22, 1952. Reprinted by permission.

stretches 1,500 miles from Minnesota to the Delaware River. But while a ton of American iron ore moves freely from say, Duluth to Pittsburgh, a ton of Ruhr coal moving 150 miles to a Lorraine steel mill is subject to half a dozen barriers including "double pricing" under which the French buyer might pay more than a German buyer, German export quotas, French import quotas and French customs duties.

The Schuman treaty will remove all these barriers to free trade. It will create one single, free market of 150 million Europeans in the six countries for coal and steel—just as the United States comprises one market. The great European coal and steel monopolies which for years have controlled production, rigged prices and carved up markets will be broken. The result—it is hoped—will be more competition, greater efficiency and therefore increased production and lower prices.

The European Coal and Steel Community will be run by an international organization. At the heart will be the nine-man supranational High Authority which will represent the whole community. The authority will have power to impose taxes, finance improvements in unprofitable enterprises, issue orders to modernize plants, increase production, lower prices that are out of line, improve wages and working conditions.

National interests will be represented by the Council of Ministers composed of members of the six participating governments. Some decisions by the Authority will be subject to majority approval by the Council, others to unanimous approval.

Political interests will be represented by a seventy-eight-man Common Assembly, which meets once a year to review the Authority's work. Its main power is that it can, by a two-thirds vote, force the members of the Authority to resign.

Finally, there will be a seven-man Court of Justice to hear appeals from states or enterprises from the decisions of the Authority.

The next step in making the treaty operative takes place later this month when the six foreign ministers meet to set up this machinery and pick the members of the High Authority. If all goes on schedule, the treaty will be in effect by July 1.

But a good many difficulties must be overcome before the integrated free-trade community becomes a reality. There are problems of personnel, of trade relations with nations outside the community, of shifts of production from high cost to low cost enterprises, of gradual adjustments of trade barriers within the community so that no one nation will be badly hurt. The treaty provides for a five-year transition period to accomplish all this.

The question of how quickly and how successfully these problems will be resolved will depend largely upon the other great Western European integration project—the European Defense Community. At present the EDC treaty is locked up in the parliaments of the six nations—none of the members has yet ratified it. A real battle over the European army plan could arouse enough distrust to block further progress on the Schuman Plan. Therefore the fate of a Coal and Steel Community rests to a large extent upon what happens in Bonn and Paris to the EDC agreement.

EUROPEAN DEFENSE COMMUNITY [7]

The reorganization of Europe, in which the Federal Republic of Germany has become a partner of the free world, reached its provisional climax in Paris . . . [May 27, 1952]. There . . . six Continental nations signed a fifty-year treaty which establishes under special guarantees from the United States and Britain, an indissoluble European Defense Community with supranational prefederal authorities, and at the same time provides for further measures looking toward the creation of an ultimate European federation modeled after the United States.

The signing of the new treaty, which marks the farthest advance toward European unification thus far, took place amid ominous rumblings from behind the Iron Curtain threatening force to frustrate its purposes. But the time has long since past that Soviet frowns could paralyze the West into hypnotic inactivity, and the Western powers, while emphasizing the purely defensive character of the new pact, not only went ahead with

[7] From "Toward a New Europe," editorial. New York *Times*. p28. May 28, 1952. Reprinted by permission.

the project but also served notice on the Soviets that any attack on any member of the new Europe they are building, or on Berlin, will be regarded as an attack on all and will be met accordingly.

Under the new treaty the six Continental signatories—France, Germany, Italy, Belgium, the Netherlands and Luxembourg—agree to integrate their military resources in the first international army ever formed in peacetime to assure their own common defense and that of the whole North Atlantic community in harmony with the United Nations Charter. This army, which will comprise around a million men organized in fifty-five divisions (or "groupements," as the French prefer to call them), including twelve German divisions, will serve shoulder to shoulder with the forces of the United States and Britain under the supreme command of NATO. But it will also be governed by the supranational authorities of the European Defense Community, which parallel and in part overlap the similar institutions of the European Coal and Steel Community, which is to provide the economic basis for it. The new army will wear the same uniform, receive the same training and pay, carry the same standardized equipment and arms and apply the same "common doctrine" based on the concepts of peace and freedom.

In all these respects the new army truly represents something new under the sun. But because it is new and is exposed to all the strains and stresses of persistent national rivalries, fears and suspicions, special precautions are taken to prevent its disintegration through defection, with a particularly stern eye on Germany. The divisions will, of necessity, be national units, but they will be unable to act independently because they will be dependent for their maintenance on multinational army corps with multinational commands and staffs. Furthermore, no heavy equipment or arms, including aircraft and large ships, will be permitted to be built in "strategically exposed" areas, meaning Germany. Finally, to allay all remaining French fears, the United States and Britain undertake, in a special protocol, not only to keep troops on the Continent as long as necessary but also to regard any action from "whatever quarter" threatening the integrity or unity of the Defense Community as a threat to their own security, and to take action of their own under the North Atlantic Treaty. In return Germany receives the same security guarantees as all other members of the North Atlantic alliance, though for the present it will not be a member of it.

It has long been recognized, however, that the European economic and defense communities now being organized will endure only if they are quickly followed by the creation of a political superstructure with more authority than the organs now established. For that reason the treaty provides that the provisional Assembly of the European Defense Community shall within six months make proposals for a permanent Assembly to succeed it and to become one of the elements of an ultimate federal or confederal structure founded on the principle of separation of powers and a bicameral system of representation. If approved by the respective governments, these are charged to call within three months a conference to examine the proposal. This plan does not go as far as the immediate calling of a constituent assembly to draft a constitution for a united Europe, as proposed by General Eisenhower. But it is along the same line, and in the long run that provision may prove to be the most important part of the whole treaty.

CARTELS VERSUS EUROPEAN INTEGRATION [8]

The Economic and Social Council of the United Nations has on the agenda . . . discussion of the international cartel agreements. It was originally planned to entrust this matter to the International Trade Organization, whose proposed charter contained provisions for international action against all agreements in restraint of trade. Since the charter did not receive the necessary support in Congress and the whole ITO project had to be shelved, the United States Government has decided to take up the fight in the Economic Council of the United Nations. Following an American suggestion, a committee of ten membernations was established to study the problem and prepare a

[8] From "How Necessary Are Cartels?" by Vaclav E. Mares, Assistant Professor of Economics, Pennsylvania State College. *Current History*. 21:331-6. December 1951. Reprinted by permission.

plan for effective control of existing cartels and, as far as possible, for their liquidation.

Although endorsed in principle by all the Marshall Plan countries, the actual elimination of restrictive business practices from trade seems to have met many obstacles in Europe. American efforts devoted to this part of the European recovery program have been largely frustrated by group agreements establishing quotas for production, sales or export shipments or keys for pooling various costs or profits according to many private, national or international trade control schemes. . . . Even those Europeans who always showed a sincere admiration for the achievements of the American free enterprise system are surprisingly united in their misgivings about the application of unlimited competition to their economies. . . .

Opening the doors to free competition might force out of production one half or more of the industrial plants which, since the days of their founding, have always been operated under the protection of some group agreements. Even if there were no other obstacles, the respective governments could hardly master the social consequences that such an action would entail. Thus it would be unrealistic to expect that the European governments, even while endorsing American views in principle, would be eager to put them into effect. Moreover, those who contended that Europe's dwindling resources had been wasted by competition in the past would oppose action in its favor. Those who hope [for] or expect growing trends toward socialization will try to maintain existing agreements for reasons of administrative expediency. Finally, there will be those who will argue that such industrial group agreements provide the only basis for moving on solid ground toward an integrated European Union.

These facts and considerations will determine the decisions of Europeans about their active participation in the new American anti-cartel drive. Even if out of deference to American views they are not advanced by the Europeans, they will remain in the background of their thinking. Formal statements of leading European politicians endorsing the American action in principle do not mean much. They are either presented as lip-service to the cherished pet-ideas of a partner from whom many favors still are needed or expected, or they are honestly meant but vaguely-formulated policy statements which are, however, not based on actual facts and are far from a practical solution.

Private and public vested interests in thousands of existing group agreements are so strong and deeply rooted in Europe's economy that, even if officially denounced, they will continue to be the driving or regulating forces of European production and trade. To be effective, their liquidation will have to be preceded by a fair, all-continental solution of the problems of resettling people, finding them new jobs, compensating for prematurely scrapped investments and making the many additional adjustments necessitated by competitive elimination of inefficient plants and industrial areas. National or regional action may help but will not solve these problems. Only a United Europe can do it on an all-continental scale. Only then, when all its industrial equipment is overhauled and geographically redistributed strictly in terms of economic rationality, can we expect Europe to be willing to accept the American challenge and open the door to free competition.

PARADOX OF UNITED STATES POLICY AND PRACTICE [9]

The cynics who told Europe that the United States would never follow through on the programs it had initiated seem, to a growing number of Europeans, to have been right.

Britain has added her voice to those of the Continental countries to remind the United States politely but firmly that American import restrictions and threats of new import restrictions violate United States commitments under international agreements, negate United States statements of its own international economic interests and threaten to nullify completely the progress Europe has made during the past few years toward a reasonable degree of economic balance with the world.

It was an essential part of the Marshall Plan that Europe should earn its way by increasing production and selling abroad more of what its farms and factories produce.

[9] From "Europeans See a Paradox in U.S. Trade Restrictions," by Michael L. Hoffman, New York *Times* Geneva correspondent. New York *Times*. p E4. April 27, 1952. Reprinted by permission.

In particular, Europe was urged, begged and tempted to sell more for dollars. Visions of the great United States markets were held before European eyes, dollar export drives were organized, bands of businessmen were transported to the United States and lectured to on their undue timidity in salesmanship and market research.

With the encouragement of their governments and prodding from American representatives in Europe, some European businessmen and merchants decided to ignore the cynics. They spent money on advertising. They refashioned products to meet American tastes. They invested in branch offices and sales representatives in the United States.

They were encouraged by tariff reductions on some imports into the United States. The United States took the lead in forming the International Trade Organization and in promoting the General Agreement on Tariffs and Trade which both the United States and the Western European countries have signed. Europe was told that these tariff reductions would stand unless serious damage was seen to be caused by floods of imports. The United States said it would not use quotas to restrict imports and objected to other countries doing so except in emergencies to protect their monetary reserves. The United States said it would simplify its customs laws, which often exclude goods for capricious reasons.

By 1951 Europe had increased sales to the United States by about 30 per cent. All of Europe's exports to the United States, however, still amounted to a paltry $100 million a month—1/230 of our monthly national income.

It is because even the modest success in increasing dollar exports has led to a wave of new protectionism in Congress and among American business groups affected by import competition that Europe is now disturbed.

"British exporters," the British Government said in its memorandum, "are perturbed by the mounting evidence that any marked success in selling their goods in the United States will be countered by applications from United States industry for further protection and the fear that at least some of these applications may be granted."

The record tends to support these fears. After five years of promises by the Administration, Congress still has not passed any customs simplification law. The United States has not joined the International Trade Organization. Unilaterally and in violation of the General Agreement on Tariffs and Trade, the United States slapped quotas on imports of cheese, milk products and casein, thus at one blow crippling the major dollar-earning industries in Italy, Denmark, the Netherlands, Norway and New Zealand. . . .

The feeling in Europe is this: If, under one kind of escape clause or another, United States producers are to be guaranteed that any product which proves itself marketable in the United States can be produced in the United States behind a protective wall high enough to overcome the difference in European and American costs, Europe will never be able to earn enough dollars to enable it to enter fully into a trading community with the United States based on a principle of nondiscrimination.

From the European point of view the root of the problem is the American belief that it is right and necessary to exclude products of "cheap labor." If products of labor that is "cheap" in dollar terms (meaning that it would be cheap if it were in the United States) are to be kept out, Europe does not have a chance.

Its only hope is in making and selling products that are uneconomical to produce in the United States, without high protection, precisely because American labor is so very much more productive than European labor in so very many industrial lines and therefore so much more expensive.

The ultimate casualties of the United States' apparently deep-seated unwillingness to permit free competition when it involves competition across frontiers are likely to be the whole of the United States sponsored commercial policy for the Western world and the institution of private enterprise in much of Western Europe. The British Government has stated quite clearly that other countries will withdraw their tariff concessions and ignore their commitments to a universal code of trade rules if the United States continues to ignore the rules itself—rules which the United States has made one of the main planks in its whole international economic platform.

Canada, the Netherlands, Denmark, Italy, France and New Zealand have made it equally plain that they will revert to a policy of every man for himself in international trade unless the United States faces the fact squarely that the world's largest creditor country cannot continue to conduct its commercial policy as if it were more important to save the "blue cheese" industry than to prevent the spread of chaos and despair in the non-Communist world.

THE SOVIET ALLIANCE SYSTEM [10]

European union proposals have been bitterly denounced by the Soviet Union and its satellites, both within and without the UN. Yet the Soviet Union commenced building its own series of alliances, directed toward building an "Eastern Union," as early as 1943. By 1949 the Soviet alliance system included mutual assistance pacts (both political and economic) with all of its satellites, and an additional seventeen pacts between individual members of the satellites themselves.

It is significant, however, that the Soviet system has been based almost wholly upon bilateral agreements between the Soviet Union and each of its satellites individually, or between satellites; whereas the Rio pact, the Brussels Treaty and the North Atlantic Treaty are all multilateral arrangements directed at "collective security."

[10] From *The Atlantic Pact*, by Halford L. Hoskins, senior specialist in international relations in the Legislative Reference Service, Library of Congress. Public Affairs Press. Washington, D.C. 1949. p92-3. Reprinted by permission.

UN, NATO, OR WORLD FEDERATION?

EDITOR'S INTRODUCTION

There are many forms of international cooperation. The simplest perhaps is the informal working relationship of two or more countries acting together. No treaty or written guarantee is required, for example, to assure United States-Canadian cooperation in many areas. It is often to the mutual advantage of nations to work together, so no formal arrangement may be neccessary. Since such working relationships are extremely rare, more conventional means are used in the majority of cases. These may take the form simply of a bilateral treaty between two nations, agreeing to common understanding on certain matters. More recently we have seen the mushroom growth of the multilateral agreement—treaties in which a number of nations reach common agreement for certain purposes. These treaties, whether bilateral or multilateral, pledge a nation to act in accordance with the treaty provisions as long as the treaty is in force. Such treaties may cover a multitude of specific subjects ranging from the definition of fishing rights in certain areas to the more publicized military alliance for the purpose of national defense.

International organizations are almost always based upon some sort of multilateral treaty which defines the obligations and limitations of nations which are members of the organization. It is the treaty which spells out in detail the form and functions of the organization. While it is frequently asserted that the form of organization is relatively unimportant and that only results count, at the present time the question centers around the form of international organization which this country should support. And since most people are in agreement as to the long-range goals of American foreign policy, it is the method by which we can best achieve these goals that concerns us here.

It should be emphasized, however, that it may be dangerous to limit the choices too much. Current discussion has generally involved only three possibilities: Keeping the United Nations as it is but attempting to strengthen it through the organization itself; carrying the United Nations idea a step further and making it over into a world federation of nations; or getting out of the United Nations entirely, relying upon alliances and regional groupings for protection. But the problem can scarcely be resolved simply by adopting one of these three programs. For one thing, regional organizations such as the Organization of American States and NATO are provided for under the UN Charter. So it is possible to have regional organizations but to depend heavily upon the United Nations in matters not pertinent to the region, or to develop regional organizations without regard to the UN and to place all reliance upon such arrangements.

An interesting sidelight on the problems of organization is the need to consider other possible members of such organizations besides the United States. Who would join us in each case? And how much support for each choice could we depend upon from member-states? The fact that these questions have had unrealized implications may be seen in the current trend toward commonwealth arrangements on the part of Britain, France and the Netherlands. All of the old colonial powers who have reluctantly "given up" their empires at the behest of UN pressure (and the threat of internal revolt) have developed commonwealth groupings involving their former colonies in an attempt to hold the colonial peoples in the economic and political sphere of influence of the mother country. The question has often been raised as to what the British position would be in any strong regional organization if the demands of that organization conflicted with British obligations under her Commonwealth arrangement. And with more countries joining in the commonwealth scheme, how can a European federation ever remain purely European? And likewise, in the UN, what is to prevent members of a commonwealth being forced into the role of satellite states such as those of Eastern Europe? The United States has already run afoul of one aspect of this problem in the Mediterranean. In the case of Israel, Iran, Egypt and Tunisia, the United States policies of encouragement of political self-determinism or independence clashed sharply with the national policies of our NATO allies, Britain and France. In the Tunisian affair, France

quite openly has stated that unless the United States supports
the French position in the UN France will withdraw from the
UN. And the Arab-Latin American coalition in the UN has
openly charged that American support of colonial imperialism
will soon destroy the UN. What form of international organization can lead us out of this type of dilemma?

Again, we are accustomed to dealing with nations in our
foreign affairs. We think of a nation in terms of a certain area
of land, usually contiguous territory, in which a majority of the
people have language, culture and interests in common. Also,
we usually think of a nation as being normally self-supporting.
But then we find today some exceedingly peculiar exceptions to
the . rule—exceptions which in their peculiarity create added
problems for organization. There is Pakistan, which is actually
two land-areas with no communication between them except by
air, but with one government. There is the first UN national
product—Libya, which cannot support itself and must depend
for many years to come upon gifts from the United States and
Britain. Then there is the newly established Maldive Kingdom
—some 2,000 islands in the Indian Ocean, whose only industry
is fishing and whose only market is India. And the list could
be expanded. Such unconventional and problem countries require special consideration when we discuss an international organization which will presumably be open to all nations. What
type of organization would be most conducive to the full, free
national expression of such nations? What are the obligations
of the United States toward such countries? Is the answer the
United Nations? Or regional pacts such as NATO? Or full
world federation?

CONGRESSIONAL REVIEW OF INTERNATIONAL ORGANIZATION [1]

As the Eighty-second Congress convened, the crisis in international organization appeared to be reaching a climax. . . .

Americans . . . have discovered that the United Nations
cannot automatically guarantee peace as many had hoped. Their

[1] From "Congress and the United Nations," by Carl Marcy, staff associate, and
Francis O. Wilcox, chief of staff, of the Senate Committee on Foreign Relations.
Foreign Policy Reports. 27:50-60. May 15, 1951. Reprinted by permission.

deep concern has been reflected by their representatives in Congress. During the Eighty-first Congress over a hundred members of the House of Representatives and more than forty Senators sponsored resolutions calling for changes in the United Nations to increase its ability to meet aggression, or for the development of other international machinery strong enough to assure peace.

[In] the Eighty-second Congress . . . a resolution . . . [was] introduced by Senator Estes Kefauver, Democrat of Tennessee, and twenty-six other senators calling upon the President to invite representatives from the North Atlantic states to explore how far their peoples can apply among them the principles of free federal union. . . .

During the spring and summer of 1950 a subcommittee of the Senate Committee on Foreign Relations, chaired by Senator Elbert D. Thomas, Democrat of Utah, gave careful consideration to some seven resolutions suggesting various ways to strengthen international organization.

The Thomas subcommittee did not recommend Senate approval of any specific proposal, believing that public opinion was not yet sufficiently crystallized to warrant such action. . . . Since 1945 the number of people who had doubts as to whether a real system of collective security was created at San Francisco grew in number. During the past year, and largely as the result of aggression in Korea, disillusionment with the United Nations has risen to alarming proportions. This disillusionment has made some people want to push ahead full steam to make the United Nations into a true world government. For others it has meant that a strong regional organization for collective defense must be created immediately. And, finally, for others a question has been raised as to whether the security of the United States should be tied up with any collective security organization outside the Western Hemisphere.

Senator Patrick A. McCarran, Democrat of Nevada, recently was quoted as believing that the United States should "pull out of the UN quickly, while there is yet time to save this country." In somewhat the same vein Senator James O. Eastland, Democrat of Mississippi, introduced a resolution calling for United States withdrawal from the United Nations if Communist China is admitted to membership.

In the months ahead, debate about American participation in the United Nations will probably deal with specific proposals. Fundamentally, however, the issue is whether the United States can best assure its own security by building a strong United Nations, by placing more emphasis on the creation of strength in the Atlantic community, and other regional groupings, or by relying on the defense capacities of the Western Hemisphere.

If the United States should either withdraw from the United Nations or should stay in the United Nations as now constituted, no very complicated domestic problems would be raised. If either of these two policies were followed, the big problem that would face the United States would be of an international character—whether this country would have firm, helpful and reliable allies in the event of war. Withdrawal from the United Nations would surely mean the loss of possible allies. Continuation in the United Nations as constituted might mean more allies. It would also impose certain restrictions on the ability of the United States to act as its own interests might dictate, without any real assurance that other members of the United Nations would take effective action against aggression.

If the United States, on the other hand, seeks a greatly strengthened United Nations or an Atlantic union or a world federation, our people must be prepared to sacrifice some degree of national independence for the advantages that would presumably accrue to us. If the United States continues on the path of collective security with its emphasis on multilateral diplomacy, we must be prepared to accept the decisions of an organization even though those decisions might at times seem to run counter to immediate United States interests.

The authors believe that the security of the United States depends in large part on the number and geographic position of reliable allies. In turn, the security of these allies depends on their willingness to stick together in the face of a common danger. All of the resolutions that have been considered propose different ways of bringing together as large a collection as possible of national states willing to use their combined strength to organize the world for peace and, if necessary, to oppose aggression with international force.

The members of the United Nations may, in the months ahead, determine whether we can have world-wide collective security in our time. The United States, as the most powerful member of that organization, will carry a heavy responsibility for the decisions that may be reached. Americans are generally agreed that the end or goal of our foreign policy should be the achievement of peace and security and the maintenance of our freedom. They are also in general agreement that the free world is threatened by Russian and Communist aggression. They believe that strength must be built to meet this threat.

There is some disagreement among Americans, however, as to the best means to achieve strength to meet aggression and preserve freedom—particularly on a long-range basis. . . . Simply defined, this disagreement is as to whether the United States should place primary emphasis upon the global, regional or hemispheric approach in its quest for collective security. The great debate in the months . . . ahead will be on this issue. Questions relating to the nature and extent of foreign military and economic assistance and to the composition of our armed force will be influenced by this debate. In fact, there is some danger that we may find the main issue settled by the day-to-day decisions on these smaller problems.

The decision which must be made, and the sooner the better, will be influenced by such diverse factors as the attitude of other members of the United Nations, including the Soviet satellite states, the attitude of Western Europe and Germany, and by debate and discussion in our country.

The decision will determine whether the United Nations is to become a relatively impotent bystander in the conflict the world faces or a more positive instrument of peace and security.

Superficially it may appear that the future of the United Nations depends on the decision of the United States. In one sense it does, for surely the course of the state that contributes nearly 40 per cent of the funds available to the United Nations and 90 per cent (excluding South Korean contributions) of the manpower for the United Nations forces in Korea will to a very great extent determine the destiny of the United Nations. But the fact is that there is a growing body of opinion in the United

States reflected in Congress which believes the course the United States must follow will depend in part on the attitude of the other members of the United Nations. If they are willing to make substantial sacrifices on their own, if they will eschew appeasement, if they recognize the true threat to world peace as Russian and Communist aggression, then the people of the United States can continue to view the United Nations as the cornerstone of this nation's foreign policy and continue to seek ways to strengthen that organization, thereby giving the ideal of collective security the support it needs to survive.

On the other hand, this group believes that if members of the United Nations are unable to make decisions, if they compromise on principles, if they view expediency as a virtue, then the United States may find it necessary, just as any other state which feels its security is endangered, to look elsewhere than to the United Nations for strength.

Thus in a very real sense, the decisions made by the United Nations and by this government, which is influenced by the thinking of the Eighty-second Congress, will determine to a large extent the suitability of proposals to strengthen international organization as devices for meeting the fundamental ideological conflict that may be with us for the next decade.

A REALISTIC VIEW OF THE UN [2]

The United Nations has been the victim of free advertising, by well-meaning, but over enthusiastic and inexperienced, friends. The United Nations ought never to have been portrayed as a mechanism which could guarantee peace. . . . Of course, we all hoped that there would be a large degree of great power unity, but history taught that this was not likely and consequently that the United Nations would probably have to depend primarily on moral power to persuade, and not on legal power to command. But such modest appraisals were drowned out by those who shouted the exciting news that, at long last, there was a world

[2] From "Reputation and Performance in World Affairs," address before the Brand Names Foundation, New York City, April 12, 1949, by John Foster Dulles, then United States delegate to the General Assembly of the UN. *Vital Speeches of the Day.* 15:465-8. May 15, 1949. Reprinted by permission.

organization guaranteed to keep the peace. Now that that is seen not to be the case, many are greatly surprised and greatly disappointed. . . . Some would junk it altogether. Others want to take it apart and try to make it over. . . .

The truth is that in the present state of the world it is not possible to remodel the United Nations into being what it was at first advertised. . . . The law-making, police-enforcing process never works unless the laws reflect the views of the community to which they apply. . . . In the world today . . . there are many different and competing faiths and there are strong anti-religious groups. In consequence, there are many different conclusions as to the facts and there are great differences of moral judgment. At the moment, nearly one third of the human race is under a system that reflects opinions very different from ours as to the nature of man and of government. . . .

The present enthusiasts for world government assume a system of weighted voting so that we and our friends, even though a minority, will control the world government. They dare not suggest that we should subject ourselves to majority rule that could readily be communistic. It is equally fantastic to suppose that Communist leaders would voluntarily subject themselves to the kind of government that we would feel to be right. Under present conditions, world government would inevitably represent an effort by some to get the power to impose upon others conditions that the others would not accept voluntarily. . . . World government, today, would be world war.

These are realities which explain why the United Nations is what it is. The inadequacy is not in the United Nations; it is in conditions outside the United Nations. . . . The United Nations, even as it is, is indispensable in the present state of the world. It is, above all, a Town Meeting of the World, where . . . differences . . . are talked about and discussed, and where slowly, but . . . surely, progress is being made toward finding common denominators of moral judgment and world opinion on which acceptable world law can gradually be built. . . .

Debate is the first stage in the process whereby men move freely toward agreement. The "town meeting" has played a great role in developing in this country the public opinion which has come to be reflected in law and order. It is the process whereby the peoples of the world can develop common judgments which may later on be reflected in world law and order. . . . Every major debate in the United Nations Assembly has brought about changes of opinion so that there was a larger measure of agreement. . . . Often the debates and discussions have helped to settle dangerous conflicts. . . . I have in mind the good progress made toward the solution of controversies such as have arisen between Israel and the Arab states, between India and Pakistan, between the Netherlands and the Indonesian Republic. . . . In these cases, as well as in many others, the processes of discussion, persuasion and appeal to the force of public opinion are producing positive results. . . .

The debates . . . have often brought about clarifications which have shifted the disagreement from an emotional to an intellectual basis. That has greatly enlarged the possibility of avoiding a violent, head-on collision. . . .

The United Nations serves to prevent nations expanding their power by fraud and trickery. Soviet leadership has attempted, through self-advertisement, to gain the reputation of providing what most people want. It seems that they consult their experts in public relations and propaganda and get their opinion as to what is the phrase or slogan that carries the most widespread popular appeal. Then they adopt that, wholly without regard to whether it corresponds with the facts, and make a tremendous, world-wide effort by radio, by press and by word of mouth to identify themselves with it. . . . That process has some success at first. But as the delegates at the United Nations have come together at their "town meeting" and have told each other of their experiences, a single pattern has been exposed and it has been seen that the government which has attempted by propaganda to get the reputation of being a "peace lover" was, in fact, the government that was teaching its followers throughout the world the use of violence and making plans for overthrowing the existing order by resort to political strikes, sabotage and civil war.

The meetings of the United Nations have thus brought to light the difference between the reputation which was advertised, and actual performance. In the case of the Soviet Union the goods do not correspond with the label. The exposure of that fact has been of tremendous importance. It has led to a solidarity against the efforts of Soviet communism which is bringing Soviet leaders to realize that they cannot, by fraudulent means, achieve their world-wide ambitions. It has greatly decreased the possibility of Soviet domination by their preferred method of indirect aggression.

Despite such very great contributions to security and to international understanding, the United Nations obviously does not wholly satisfy the reasonable desire of the member-states for security against direct aggression. That desire, we have seen, cannot now be satisfied on a universal basis. It can, however, be measurably satisfied through the organization for collective self-defense of groups of nations that have common views as regards the fundamental values that are worth defending. . . . We are now in the process of consummating in treaty form a unity of the so-called West, which has common traditions and a common heritage for which, indeed, we have twice fought great wars.

There exist other natural associations of peoples who are bound together by tradition and a sense of values held in common. Of these, the British Commonwealth of Nations is an outstanding example.

These are ways in which people draw together in unity to find the increased strength and security which flow from unity. The essential is an underlying sense of community. On this foundation a political structure can be erected which at first may be informal and loose, but which can be elaborated and formalized if, in fact, the foundation is solid.

These processes are not forbidden by the United Nations Charter. It would, indeed, be folly if the United Nations prevented international growth except at the universal level where progress is, inevitably, the most slow. The fact is that the Charter authorizes collective self-defense and encourages regional associations.

There is, of course, always a danger that groups of states will develop a power which may tempt them to act in ways which impair the general welfare and jeopardize the peace. . . . It is not, however, necessary to stop the natural processes of growth and unification merely because they give an increased strength that might be abused. It is up to the peoples who make up the union to make sure that it will be operated in ways such that freedom from fear within the group is not achieved at the expense of giving others valid reason to be fearful. . . .

The task of achieving world order is at once so difficult and so urgent that it is necessary to tackle it from every angle. No single approach is of itself enough. It is important, wherever practical, to end the disunity and political isolation which exposes the weaker nations to aggression by ambitious and powerful despots. It is equally important to have a world organization which will bring all the nations of the world together for discussion, for exposure and for judgment at the bar of world opinion.

So far as the United Nations is concerned, there is no reason to join the ranks either of those who would try to turn it into world government or who would abandon it as useless. Experience since the San Francisco Conference points to these two conclusions: First, if the United Nations had been established as the highly powered world government organization that many thought it was, we would probably by now, be in a world war. Secondly, if there had been no United Nations at all, then indirect aggression would have proceeded without effective resistance, until the free societies were so reduced in number and so closely encircled that they would have felt impelled to fight their way out of an ever tightening noose. . . . Therefore, I submit, the inevitable process of shedding illusions about the United Nations should not drive us either to abandon the United Nations or to attempt unrealistically to make it over. Rather, it is an occasion for a sober reappraisal of the United Nations and a demonstration to use to the full its real rather than its imaginary possibilities.

ALTERNATIVES TO THE UN [3]

What is surprising to me is not that the United Nations has not been able to achieve more than it has . . . but that it has been able to achieve as much as it has. . . . I often ask myself this question: Would the world situation during the past four years have been better, if the United Nations did not exist? I doubt it. . . .

Nevertheless, it is quite understandable that public discussion of the United Nations, especially in this country, has been strongly marked by a note of disappointment and disillusionment. This feeling has been strengthened to a large extent by the unfortunate fact that, when the United Nations was created, there was a general tendency to expect much more from it than it could possibly deliver. It should have been crystal clear from the start that the new international organization could not be expected to transform the whole system of relations among nations. Unfortunately, emerging as the world was from the holocaust of a terrible war, there were too many people who were carried away by the idea that the mere establishment of an international organization would perform the miracle of taking care of all our troubles.

The truth of the matter was that by establishing the United Nations the peace-seeking nations of the world were providing themselves with a new and important mechanism for the conduct of international relations, but one that was to be supplementary to all the other machinery of international relations, rather than one that would entirely supplant the latter. After all, the United Nations is not something suspended in the air above the nations themselves. The United Nations is the nations that compose it. It can help the nations to raise the standards of their international behavior, but it cannot rise above the standards set by the nations themselves. I cannot imagine a situation in which the nations would behave like

[3] From "Revision of the United Nations Charter"; hearings, February 2-20, 1950; statement before the Senate Foreign Relations Committee by Leo Pasvolsky, Director, International Studies Group, Brookings Institution. Superintendent of Documents. Washington, D.C. 1950. p739-41.

angels in the United Nations and be at each others' throats outside the United Nations, or vice versa. . . .

There is always, naturally, a search for simple and direct solutions, no matter how complicated the problems are that clamor for solution. Hence, it is entirely understandable that the existing widespread feeling of disillusionment and frustration has led to a vigorous search for other ways out, and that many proposals have been devised for changing the United Nations system, or, as the current phrase runs, for "strengthening" the United Nations.

One such proposal . . . is to reorganize the United Nations without the Soviet Union and its satellites. I can well understand the feeling of utter exasperation with the Soviet Union's methods of behavior that makes such a procedure attractive. But I see no useful purpose to be served by deliberately releasing Soviet Russia from the obligations that it assumed when it accepted the Charter of the United Nations. On the contrary, I can see the possibility of using its signature on the Charter, however dishonored by its present behavior, as a basis for moral pressure against it. I can also see the possibility that renewed adherence to the principles of international behavior inscribed on the Charter may become a bridge by which Soviet Russia may return to the family of nations once its leaders come to the conclusion that the road they are following now can lead only to disaster. And I would be inclined to deplore our shutting the door, by this act of ostracism, on the desperate hopes of the peoples who are under the despotic rule of the leaders of Moscow.

The proponents of the proposal are not quite clear on what would be accomplished by such an action. . . . Apart from this proposal, most of the others center around ways of revising the existing organization. The one that is perhaps oftenest heard of is based on the idea that the abolition, or at least substantial modification, of the veto privilege would sufficiently strengthen the United Nations to make it a really effective instrument for the maintenance of peace and security. Let us take a look at what would happen if this were done.

Obviously, if no single nation were in a position to stop, by its vote alone, any decision of the United Nations, a very important limitation on action by the United Nations would be removed. The United Nations would then be in a situation in which, if the requisite majorities could be obtained, it would be able not only to condemn any aggressor—this it can do now through the General Assembly, where the veto does not apply—but also to make a decision to act against any member-state, including the major nations.

But would such a decision have any reality? The United Nations would still have to have the means of enforcing it. If the theory is correct that a major nation can be coerced only by a combination of the forces of the other major nations, this would mean that the United Nations would have to have the authority to call into action, if necessary, all of the forces and resources of all the major nations not accused of crimes and misdemeanors. Hence, the abolition of the veto would have significance only if this second step were taken—specifically, if the United States were willing to permit the United Nations, by a majority vote, to call into action American armed forces, even at a time when its representatives had voted against the action.

Those who advocate the abolition or mitigation of the veto as the solution to all our problems must, I think, first make reasonably sure that the American people are prepared—as I am sure they were not five years ago—to accept such an arrangement.

The abolition or modification of the veto provision requires an amendment of the Charter, and such an amendment can become effective only if two thirds of the member states agree to it and if that majority includes the concurrent votes of all the permanent members of the Security Council. This fact has led some advocates of strengthening the United Nations to devise a proposal based on the idea of getting around the veto. Specifically, it is proposed that a pact supplementary to the Charter be negotiated and that its signatories obligate themselves to consider an attack on any one of them as an attack on itself and to come to the assistance of the state attacked. This obligation would come into effect when a determination that an attack had taken place is made, either by the Security Council under its present procedures or by a two-thirds vote of the General Assembly, provided that the Assembly's vote includes the concurrence of at least three of the five permanent members of the Security Council.

This proposal again involves the fundamental issue that I have just mentioned in connection with the abolition of the veto. By adhering to such a pact, the United States would have to accept the obligation to use its forces and resources on the decisions of other nations, in the event that it happened to be one of the two major nations voting in the negative on the action to be taken. I shall not stop to discuss the many great difficulties that this proposal presents, but I should like to make this observation. In the two regional security pacts into which the United States recently entered—the Rio Treaty and the North Atlantic Treaty—this country refused to accept a situation in which its forces and resources could be used for collective action, except on its own decision. I sometimes wonder what reason the proponents of this idea have for believing that this country would be willing to give a majority of the United Nations the kind of authority that it has so far denied to the other twenty American republics and to the other eleven members of the North Atlantic group. . . .

Proposals for improving the functioning of the United Nations by eliminating or mitigating the veto privilege represents . . . an attack on the symptom rather than the disease. That disease is rooted in the general state of world affairs, and especially in the current profound split among the major nations, rather than in any structural features of the United Nations. In any event, the veto provision cannot be altered so long as the split exists. . . .

There is another group of proposals that go even further. They involve the transformation of the United Nations into a system of world government, either on a federal or unitary basis. These proposals are not new. When we were working on the Charter of the United Nations, some highly articulate groups urged upon us the idea that the principle of voluntary association should be abandoned in favor of the principle of supernational government. There was a time when this pressure became sufficiently strong to make it necessary for President Roosevelt and Secretary Hull to reassure the country that we were not seeking a system of supergovernment, for at that time, the principal effects of the pressure were to arouse widespread fears that the United States might be led into an organization based on the supergovernment principle.

Those who worked on the Charter were convinced that the real issue was not between the relative merits of the two basic principles of organization. The real issue was whether it was possible to create any kind of a world organization to which all of the peace-seeking nations, and especially the major nations, would be willing to adhere. It was felt that if the world-government idea had been put on the agenda of international negotiations, no success was likely to emerge.

But apart from the question whether the creation of a system of world government is feasible, desirable, or even likely to do what its proponents claim for it . . . what again concerns me at this moment is whether the American people would or should enter into an arrangement in which the nation's armed forces and resources could be used without its consent. And let us remember that a world government system would have to mean much more than that. It would involve the right of such a government to conscript American citizens, to tax American citizens, to regulate immigration, to bring an American citizen before a world court, and to do a great many other things that would need to be done if such a government were to function. The proponents of the scheme assure us that all they are thinking of is a world government endowed with defined and limited powers to maintain international peace and security. I am afraid that no matter how much you "define" or how much you "limit" the powers of a world government called upon to perform the tasks involved, there would be precious little left that would be really substantial of the powers now possessed by the Government of the United States or of any other country entering into such a system.

There are some proponents of a change who urge the establishment of regional governments on the federal principle. The most prominent of these is the scheme for a North Atlantic federation. The same arguments apply from the point of view of American participation as in the case of a world government, and the same problems are presented for decision to the people of the United States.

There is one point of crucial importance that I should like to note in connection with all of these proposals. They all concentrate on machinery of government and machinery of relations among nations rather than on the underlying processes of organized society. They are all based on the idea that if we could only find the right machinery, everything else would take care of itself.

I do not deny, of course, that machinery is extremely important in social organization, whether on a national, regional, or a world scale. But it ought to be clear that no machinery of government can function effectively unless back of it are the proper attitudes and human relationships necessary to its successful functioning.

Looking back over the postwar years it seems clear to me that there is plenty of machinery in the world to make peace and security living realities, if only there were back of that machinery a real determination to make it work. Details—in some cases important ones—can and should be perfected as experience points the way. The United Nations Charter was never intended to be a fixed and inflexible instrument. On the contrary, a conscious effort was made to make it an instrument capable of development and growth. The Charter itself provides for periodic reviews of the operations of the United Nations. It was originally thought that such a review might not be necessary for ten years.. Perhaps events have moved so speedily as to make such a review advisable in the near future, if for no other reason than to clarify the basic underlying issues that are now so badly distorted and confused.

But it seems to me that tinkering with the machinery of international organization as a means of solving the grave and perilous problems that confront us is merely an attempt to escape from the stubborn realities of the world in which we live. The most stubborn of those realities is that there is no easy way out. Not mechanical panaceas, but patience, hard work, ingenuity, moral and physical strength, and the will to use that strength to preserve what free men prize most, offer the only hope that mankind will win through the terrible difficulties with which it is now faced.

GIBRALTAR OF THE WEST [4]

A year ago the North Atlantic pact had been in operation for over a year. Up to that time, despite huge subsidies and sacrifices by the American people, the nations of Europe, except Britain, had done little in mutual defense. . . .

A year ago we were told that a European defense army of upward of forty ground divisions would be created under General Eisenhower by the end of 1952, with twenty more divisions by the end of 1954.

We were told four more American divisions were to be shipped to Europe in addition to the two we already had there.

What has happened?

The rearming of Western Europe is mainly dependent upon the French and the Germans. A year ago, in urging that we send our divisions, General Eisenhower stated to the Congress that the French promised fifteen battleworthy divisions by the end of 1952 and presumably more by the end of 1953. A few days ago, the French Defense Minister indicated that they contemplated only ten divisions for the European army of which none was complete and half of them were only 50 per cent recruited.

The settlement by which Western Germany is to be given a certain degree of independence and is to contribute twelve divisions has not yet gone beyond the paper stage. No battleworthy German divisions are in sight—certainly not before 1953.

[4] From "The Year Since the Great Debate," radio address by Herbert Hoover, former president of the United States. *Vital Speeches of the Day.* 18:258-61. February 15, 1952. Reprinted by permission.

The British have announced that their four divisions on the continent will not be a part of the European army but that they "will cooperate." . . .

In sum, the only substantial additions to Western European ground armies during the two years past have been the American divisions we have sent over.

Aside from American and British divisions it would be difficult to find ten battleworthy divisions in the Western European army today. And it would appear that even the sixty division army is two or three years away. . . .

A year ago, we were told that the Communist armies comprised 300 divisions, 20,000 planes and 30,000 tanks. No one contended that sixty European divisions, even if created, could do more than temporarily halt an invasion. . . .

I may say at once that all the American people are interested in the growth of unity in Continental Europe and their preparation of adequate ground armies for their defense. . . . There has been some progress during the past year in allaying age-old discords and dissensions. But they are obviously not yet cured.

Among forces which obstruct progressive Western European statesmen are the potent Socialist and Communist parties. These parties also have widely spread the belief that our subsidies and our urging are for the purpose of using Europe for American cannon fodder. Yet the Western European nations are contributing less than 10 per cent of the total military expenditures of the North Atlantic Pact Nations.

Another cause of Western European inertia is its attitude as to the risk of Communist invasion. That attitude is profoundly different from the attitude of Washington. There is in Europe today no such public alarm as has been fanned up in the United States. None of those nations has declared emergencies or taken measures comparable with ours. . . .

The outstanding phenomenon in the United States is the dangerous overstraining of our economy by our gigantic expenditures. The American people have not yet felt the full impact of the gigantic increase in Government spending and taxes. Yet we already suffer from the blight of inflation and confiscatory taxes. We are actually in a war economy except for world-wide shooting. We are diverting more and more civilian production to war materials. We are placing a greater portion of our manpower under arms. All this creates scarcity in civilian goods and increased spending power, both of which fan the flames of inflation.

We are constantly told that measures are being taken by the Government to "prevent" inflation. This ignores the fact that we are in the middle of inflationary operations at this very minute. Even since the end of the second World War the purchasing power of our money, measured in wholesale prices, has decreased 40 per cent. . . .

Under the demands of Washington we are confronted with a probable Federal deficit of $30 to $40 billions for immediate rearmament. We already have government obligations and currency of $280 billion. And private credit is dangerously over-expanded. In the brief period since the war, it has swelled by $130 billion. . . . The two pressures—scarcities and expanding credit or paper money—are the irresistible forces of inflation. They are already being expressed in gray markets and a sporadic spiral of higher wages and then higher prices. . . .

In view of this past year's experience, and these rising pressures, the Congress should again reexamine our situation.

I believe there are methods more effective to check the Communist menace in the long run and at the same time to lessen our domestic dangers.

As a basis for test I may repeat the essentials of the proposals some of us made a year ago which were supported by many military and economic authorities:

First. That the first national purpose of this republic must be the defense of this final Gibraltar of freedom—that is the Western Hemisphere.

Second. That the only way to save Europe from destruction is to avoid the third world war. The real and effective deterrent which we can, within our resources, contribute to that end is in cooperation with the British to extend our already strong air and navies up to a striking force. The Communists know that such a striking force could destroy their military potential if they started an invasion and it could punish any such aggression. And this applies to aggression against other non-Communist countries as well as Western Europe. . . .

Third. That the only way we can hold the initiative in this cold war is not to scatter our ground armies all around the 25,000 miles of Communist borders but to concentrate on such a highly mobile striking force by air and sea. . . .

Fourth. That we should furnish such munitions as we can afford to other nations who show a determined will to defend themselves.

Fifth. That to maintain the economic strength of the United States and to prevent its socialization does not permit our building up great ground armies in addition to overwhelming air and sea forces and supply of munitions to other nations. . . .

Sixth. That true friendship with Western European nations requires they be told certain things in no uncertain terms. They should realize the limit of our economic aid is this deterrent air and sea power and munitions. That, protected by this shield, we expect them, on the basis of their performance in previous wars, and now with the aid of munitions from us, to realize that ground armies are Europe's own problem. We should state that we expect them to provide ground protection to our airfields within their boundaries. We should state that not only will we send no more ground troops, but that we expect they will rapidly relieve us of that burden except to protect our airfields outside the NATO countries.

And they should be told that their delays leave our . . . European garrison [of 250,000 men] in a most exposed position.

Seventh. Our relations to the United Nations Charter should be revised. It must not be allowed to dominate the internal sovereignty of our Government. Our courts have already made decisions that the Charter overrides our domestic laws.

Recalculation of our policies along these lines would greatly reduce our economic risks. By restricting our ground armies and ultimately reducing them to the force necessary to protect our homeland and our essential air bases outside of European NATO countries, together with a reduction or postponement of 30 per cent in our Federal civil expenditures, we could assure our economic strength. We could return thousands of young men to their shops, their farms, and their colleges. We could apply real brakes upon this drift to inflation; we might stop the plunge into socialism; we could avoid increase in taxes. But above all, we could better halt the spread of Communist imperialism.

It has been said that in these evil times peace can be preserved only through strength. That is true. But the center and final reserve of strength of the free world lies in the North American continent. Nothing must be permitted to weaken this bastion. We should recalculate our risks.

THE WORLD FEDERALISTS' PROGRAM [5]

No one will disagree that we must meet the current international crises as best we can with what we have. We must use the machinery of the United Nations to cope with immediate problems that will not wait. We must support UN efforts to improve world conditions of health and welfare, and sustain its long-range programs to identify and overcome the root causes of aggression.

But this is not enough. We must give the United Nations the power through enforceable law to prevent both war and preparation for war. The moral effect of world opinion is a powerful force, but unless it is backed by an institutional structure sufficiently strong to compel a peaceful adjudication of differences and prevent an appeal to violence, it is most unlikely that world opinion alone can prevent the arms race from exploding into armed conflict.

United World Federalists advocates the transformation of the United Nations, through amendment of its Charter, from a league of fully sovereign states into a world federal government with powers limited, but adequate to assure peace. This transformation is necessary because so long as we have armed sovereign nations they can be coerced into abiding by treaties

[5] From "From UN to World Federation," by Cord Meyer, Jr., Chairman, Executive Committee, United World Federalists. *Journal of the American Association of University Women.* p 136-8. Spring 1950. Reprinted by permission.
(This article appeared in "World Organization—the next step," a symposium. It expresses the author's personal views and is not to be regarded as necessarily representing the policy or opinion of the American Association of University Women.)

only through war itself, through force of arms against a whole people. War can be prevented only by a world federation with laws which are applicable to individuals, that can be enforced peaceably and justly against the guilty alone by means of a world police force and a system of world courts.

Such a federation would require a world legislature, perhaps derived from the UN General Assembly, with representation determined upon a compromise formula recognizing the relative power of the member-states, but not based on population alone. This federation would require also an executive body, perhaps derived from the Security Council, responsible to the legislature, and operating without a veto. A system of world courts with compulsory jurisdiction over individuals as well as national governments in those matters within its competence would have to be provided, perhaps by an expansion of the present World Court.

As a minimum, this federation should have the following powers: to prohibit possession by any nation of armaments and forces beyond an approved level required for internal policing; to control the dangerous aspects of atomic energy and other scientific developments easily diverted to mass destruction; to raise dependable revenue through direct taxation; and to maintain such world inspection, police, and armed forces as may be necessary to enforce world law and provide world security.

All powers not expressly delegated to the world federal government should be reserved to the nations and their peoples, thus leaving each nation its own domestic political, economic, social, and religious institutions.

A world constitution should include a bill of rights assuring equal and adequate protection from arbitrary authority to persons affected by the constitution and laws of the world federal government, and a reasonable provision for amendment of the constitution.

An immediate declaration on the part of the United States Government that transformation of the United Nations into a limited world federation open to all nations is the fundamental objective of United States foreign policy is the first step. This would have to be followed by extensive consultations with other member governments to assess the amount and kind of agreement which could be reached. On the basis of understandings with a large majority of the UN member nations, a UN Charter review conference could be convened under Article 109 for the purpose of making this proposal to all nations, and every effort should be made to get universal agreement to it.

A partial federation within the present UN structure should be resorted to only if exhaustive efforts to get universal agreement fail. Such a partial federation could be successful in preserving peace only if it succeeded in obtaining by voluntary consent the membership of those nations which initially chose to remain outside. A partial federation would have to be armed in its own defense until such time as all nations were included.

It may seem easier to initiate a federal solution to the problem of war with our friends than with our potential enemies, but a peace plan with friendly nations alone can be nothing but a further threat which will be matched in kind. Security for either side is possible only when the conflicting interests are contained together within a system of law that effectively prohibits a resort to war as a means of settling these real differences.

Whether a majority of the American people and of their elected representatives can be persuaded in time to propose and accept the transformation of the UN into a federation is still an open question. But the fact that 22 senators and 104 representatives have introduced concurrent resolutions in the Congress calling for this step is an encouraging indication that the people are waking to the dangers they face if law cannot be substituted for force as a means of settling the disputes that must inevitably occur between nations.

WORLD FEDERATION VERSUS
ATLANTIC UNION [6]

The necessity of a federation equipped to enact and enforce world law, in the limited sphere of war prevention, is now

[6] Excerpts from statement submitted to the Foreign Affairs Committee of the House of Representatives in support of H.C.R. 64, October 17, 1949, by Grenville Clark, author and lecturer on world government. Supt of Docs. Washington, D.C. 1949.

so generally recognized as the prerequisite of disarmament and peace that I need not argue that general proposition. Rather the vital questions now are: When and how do we start? Shall the United States lead? What precisely should be the structure, powers, and membership of the federation? Specifically, should an effort be now made for universal membership or should the federation be confined, at least at the start, to the democracies?

I concentrate on the last of those issues . . . world federation . . . contemplates an effort from the start for universal membership; while . . . Atlantic Union . . . contemplates, at least at the beginning, an exclusive and partial membership. . . .

Atlantic Union . . . would materially and perhaps fatally weaken the United Nations. Even if restricted to the twelve Atlantic Pact countries, the so-called free federation would include a preponderance of the economic and military power (although less than one fourth of the population) of the world. United in a federal union with a single military establishment and constituting a single economic unit . . . it would completely overshadow the UN. That institution would almost necessarily shrink into insignificance and the prospect of developing the UN into an effective world federation would virtually disappear. If we are sincere in wishing not only to support and strengthen the UN, but to achieve its evolution into a truly effective instrument of world law and order, I submit that we cannot emphasize the world's division by seeking to create an immensely powerful separate federation whether or not within the framework of the UN, whatever that may mean. . . .

There is another and a better way to seek disarmament and peace than by attempting a partial federation "within the framework" of the United Nations. That way . . . is to seek the development of the United Nations itself "into a world federation open to all nations." It is the last four words which are the most important of all. They need not be construed to mean that if, after every reasonable effort, it proves impossible to obtain a universal federation, no lesser federation should ever be formed. But they do mean, I believe, that an effort should be made, a strong and persistent effort, to obtain universal membership. They mean that this effort shall be made to the end that the world division shall be healed and that there shall eventuate, if humanly possible, a genuine regime of world law to which shall be subject all rather than some of the nations and their people. . . .

We should never forget that however necessary our present policy under the Atlantic Treaty may be, that policy can be no more than a stopgap. It embodies no element of world order under law. On the contrary, it is the essence of power politics. It may well be helpful in gaining time to seek the solution. It is in itself no stable solution at all.

RELATION OF EDC, NATO AND UN [7]

"EDC" [European Defense Community] is a small area— let us say, a square—occupied by six nations: France, Western Germany, Italy, Belgium, the Netherlands and Luxembourg. NATO, the North Atlantic Treaty Organization, takes in all these nations except Western Germany, and adds the United States, Britain, Canada, Norway, Denmark, Iceland, Portugal and . . . Greece and Turkey. In effect, NATO is a larger square enclosing the smaller one. Finally . . . is the United Nations— sixty governments, but not including Italy, Portugal or Western Germany. . . .

THE FALLACY OF COLLECTIVE SECURITY [8]

The Korean War has naturally enough brought with it a reexamination of the United Nations. The question—whether peace can be enforced by the united actions of all other nations against an aggressor nation—is not a new one. . . .

The real issue in the discussions between 1914 and 1919 was not . . . an issue between isolationists and supporters of

[7] From "Death and Birth at Lisbon," editorial. New York *Times.* p E8. February 24, 1952. Reprinted by permission.
[8] From "Reexamining the UN," by Walter Lippmann, author, and special writer for the New York *Herald Tribune. Reader's Digest.* 60:71-2. June 1952. (Reprinted from the New York *Herald Tribune,* January 15, 1951) Reprinted by permission.

a League of Nations. The real issue was whether to base our security on an alliance primarily with Britain and France or on the general principle of collective security. There was no serious disagreement about whether there should be a universal society of all the nations. The serious question was whether we should enter this society in alliance with our best allies or whether the alliance should be dissolved and the principle of "collective security" substituted for it. . . .

The tidal wave of isolationism in the United States in the twenties was the consequence of President Wilson's decision to identify the League of Nations with the principle of collective security. There was a popular fear that the League of Nations would involve this country in endless and destructive wars.

Senator Taft in one of his speeches . . . recognized the fact that collective security is an unworkable principle, and he recommended that we "develop our own policy of military alliances without regard to the nonexistent power of the United Nations to prevent aggression." And yet he continues to support the UN as a diplomatic instrument. . . .

This is essentially the right view. . . . No universal society like the United Nations can survive if it is expected to execute the principle of collective security. The general and official view ever since President Wilson's time has been . . . that unless an international organization is able to suppress aggression by collective action it has no reason for existence. But the truth . . . is that a universal society cannot enforce peace by collective action and will be destroyed if it tries to.

The old League in respect to Manchuria and Ethiopia, the United Nations in respect to Korea and China have shown up collective security—they have shown that you cannot rally all the nations to a collective war to enforce peace.

The trouble with collective security is that, when the issue is less than the survival of the *great* nations, the method of collective security will not be used because it is just as terrifying to the policeman as it is to the lawbreakers. It punishes the law-enforcing states, at least until they have paid the awful price of victory, as much as the lawbreaking states. You can't achieve peace through law by calling upon masses of innocent people to stand ready to exterminate masses of other people. . . .

Survival of the United Nations depends . . . on a general recognition of the fact that, while it is not a policeman and cannot be made into a policeman—not even if the Russians were expelled—it is nonetheless an invaluable, indeed an indispensable, diplomatic meeting place. Were it dissolved, we should be asking where and how we can achieve general contact and diplomatic intercourse not merely with our Soviet adversaries but with the great number of states in Asia, the Middle East, Europe and Africa who are our allies or are friendly neutrals.

Let us then be careful not to sacrifice all that on the altar of the principle of collective security—which in practice is not collective and does not bring security.

THE ATLANTIC COMMUNITY DILEMMA [9]

The United Kingdom is not a participant in the proposed Schuman Plan. It has likewise indicated that it cannot fully participate in the formation of a European army. In fact . . . the position of the United Kingdom seems to be that she wishes to be "associated with" any European political federation, specialized agency, or army that the Europeans themselves may create, but does not wish to become part and parcel of any such arrangement. This attitude not only affects Britain, but also is a deterrent to Sweden, Norway, and Ireland. . . .

Aside from the vital importance of Great Britain to such a union, the fact is that during the debates in Strasbourg, the European nations almost without exception pointed to the reluctant attitude of the United Kingdom as a nearly insurmountable obstacle to unification. Of course, it is possible that if the United Kingdom did join, the other countries might find additional reasons for not going along, but the major obstacle pointed out repeatedly was that it would be difficult for such a

[9] From "The Union of Europe," report of the meetings between a delegation appointed by Congress and representatives appointed by the Consultative Assembly of the Council of Europe, November, 1951, presented by Senator Theodore Francis Green, chairman of the Senate delegation. (Senate Document no90) 82d Congress, 2d session. Superintendent of Documents. Washington, D.C. 1952. p 10-18.

union to function successfully without full participation by the United Kingdom, Norway, Sweden, and Ireland. . . .

It is likely that to some extent the British attitude is dictated by uncertainty as to the future of the Atlantic community. . . . This . . . has two aspects. In the first place many Britons are concerned about whether they should take seriously the Atlantic Union resolution which has been supported by a large number of members of Congress. Second, they are concerned about what powers, and in what way NATO is to be furnished.

One of the British delegates commented on this situation to the American delegation (at Strasbourg) as follows:

> If we are going to join an Atlantic union, we have got to bring Europe with us, otherwise you will not have us. We know that. Europe is vital; but there is also NATO, and NATO is where the real power lies, NATO is what we all depend upon for our security and existence.

This shows how seriously many Britons consider proposals regarding Atlantic Union.

There are three different European or Atlantic community international organizations which are being developed or contemplated today: The North Atlantic Treaty Organization (NATO), the Council of Europe, and the Atlantic Union. The first two of these organizations are already in existence although their powers have not been fully defined. The third, Atlantic Union, is an idea in men's minds which has such strong support in certain quarters that it influences efforts to spell out more fully the powers of NATO and the Council of Europe.

It can scarcely be said that the development of these organizational concepts has taken place in a well-ordered and coherent pattern. While each has been developed to help build strength in the free Western world, membership is (or would be in the case of Atlantic Union) different, the emphasis on the fundamental purpose of the organization is different, and the authority delegated to the organization is different.

As to membership, there is considerable overlapping between the Council of Europe and the Atlantic Pact; the main differences being that Sweden, Ireland, and Western Germany are not members of the NATO whereas NATO includes the United

States, Canada, and Portugal in its membership. Atlantic Union is more exclusive in its proposed selection of delegates to meet in a federal convention, as can be seen from the accompanying chart.

COUNCIL OF EUROPE	ATLANTIC PACT	ATLANTIC UNION †
Great Britain	Great Britain	Great Britain
France	France	France
Netherlands	Netherlands	Netherlands
Belgium	Belgium	Belgium
Luxembourg	Luxembourg	Luxembourg
Norway	Norway	
Sweden		
Denmark	Denmark	
Iceland	Iceland	
Ireland		
Italy	Italy	
Greece	Greece	
Turkey	Turkey	
Western Germany		
Saar*		
	Canada	Canada
	United States	United States
	Portugal	

* Associate member

† List taken from pending Senate resolution, which provides, however, that other states may be invited to join.

In general people think of NATO as a defense organization, the Council of Europe as a political or economic organization, and the proposed Atlantic Union as primarily political in nature. In fact, however, the North Atlantic Treaty has language broad enough to encourage some individuals to believe that it can grow into the type of organization proposed by proponents of Atlantic Union. Article 2 of the North Atlantic Treaty provides that "The parties will contribute toward the further development of peaceful and friendly international relations . . . by promoting conditions of stability and well-being" and "will seek to eliminate conflict in their international economic policies and will encourage economic collaboration between any or all of them." They are also pledged in Article 3 to "maintain and develop their individual and collective capacity to resist armed attack." This is language broad enough to be interpreted as encouraging, and perhaps authorizing, political and economic collaboration of the closest type.

The statute of the Council of Europe states that "matters relating to national defense do not fall within the scope of the Council of Europe." As a matter of practice, however, the Consultative Assembly has fully and freely discussed economic and political aspects of defense and in 1950 it adopted a resolution favoring the creation of a European army. Thus the Council is getting involved in the defense business of NATO. . . .

[Atlantic Union] . . . was described in 1950 by Mr. Justice Roberts when he appeared before a subcommittee of the Senate Foreign Relations Committee . . . [as an organization] whose powers might include (1) A union defense force and foreign policy; (2) a union free market; (3) a union currency; (4) a union postal system; (5) a union citizenship, in addition to national citizenship; and (6) a union power of taxation. . . .

The United Kingdom is caught in the midst of this maelstrom of ideas. She is a member of the Council of Europe, of NATO and would presumably be a charter member of any Atlantic Union. England draws away from any further political involvement in Western Europe. She does not know what NATO or Atlantic Union may hold for the future. She would probably rather develop close political and economic ties with the United States and the Commonwealths than with Western Europe but she is not sure of the position of the United States with respect to any of these organizational concepts.

Lord Layton posed the British dilemma in these words:

So long as we are in the realm of general terms, the mind of the public is confused. . . . If we could define the functions of NATO so that it was no longer confused with a constitutional federation of the Atlantic world, and so that there was no longer the idea that there was an alternative and greater federation in which they could join, then I believe that we should find it much easier to go ahead with the creation of a united Europe. . . .

Several years ago it was said, half in jest, that if the Soviet were to attack the West there would be no soldiers to defend the free world but there would be committees enough to provide adequate defense. Today as one looks at the political organization of Western Europe and the Atlantic community he cannot but be impressed by the organizational confusion that frustrates the creation of any coherent pattern for the development of a strong, well ordered, democratic community capable of exerting the tremendous efforts that are essential if freedom is to survive.

It may be that the organizational chaos in the North Atlantic community today is a chaos out of which order will flow. It may be but a step in the evolution of a community of free nations dedicated to the preservation of individual freedom. But the danger we face is so great that it may be fatal to wait for evolutionary processes to develop a free united Europe, or an Atlantic community, or any other combination of states that would pool some degree of sovereignty for common purposes.

It seems clear that the relationships between NATO, the Council of Europe, and the proposed Atlantic Union give rise to many questions that have not been thought through. How far does the United States propose to go with NATO? Is the United States seriously giving consideration to the type of political federation that would be involved in Atlantic Union? Are the congressional sponsors, as well as the American public, fully aware of the sovereign powers the United States would be expected to relinquish if some degree of Atlantic Union were to be adopted? Is the United States aware of the full implications of European federation? Might not such a federation, for example, strengthen Communist parties within the participating countries because they would have unified direction and at the same time weaken the democratic parties which by their very nature would not be subject to totalitarian control? Would moves involving the relinquishment of power in foreign or domestic fields raise more perplexing problems than they would solve?

BIBLIOGRAPHY

An asterisk (*) preceding a reference indicates that the article or a part of it has been reprinted in this book.

BOOKS, PAMPHLETS, AND DOCUMENTS

*American Assembly. United States—Western Europe relationships as viewed within the present world-wide international environment; discussion guide. 218p. The Assembly. Graduate School of Business. Columbia University. New York. '51.

Baldwin, H. W. The price of power. 361p. Harper & Bros. New York. '47.

Bolles, Blair and Wilcox, F. O. Armed road to peace. (Headline Series no92) 62p. Foreign Policy Association. 22 E. 38th St. New York 16. '52.

Brinton, Crane. The United States and Britain. 305p. Harvard University Press. Cambridge, Mass. '45.

Bundy, McGeorge, ed. The pattern of responsibility. 309p. Houghton Mifflin Co. Boston. '52.

Burnham, James. Struggle for the world. 248p. John Day Co. New York. '47.

Clark, Grenville. A plan for peace. 83p. Harper & Bros. New York. '50.

Danish Information Office. Scandinavian cooperation: a report to the Council of Europe. 25p. The Office. 588 Fifth Ave. New York 19. '51.

Dean, V. M. Europe and the United States. 347p. Alfred A. Knopf. New York. '50.

De Rusett, Alan. Strengthening the framework of peace. 225p. Royal Institute of International Affairs. London. '50.

Duggan, Laurence. The Americas. 242p. Henry Holt & Co. New York. '49.

Dulles, J. F. War or peace. 274p. Macmillan Co. New York. '50.

Eaton, H. O. and others. Federation—the coming structure of world government. 234p. University of Oklahoma Press. Norman. '44.

Hessler, W. H. Operation survival. 276p. Prentice-Hall. New York. '49.

Hoffman, P. G. Peace can be won. 188p. Doubleday & Co. Garden City, N.Y. '51.
The story of the ECA program.

Johnsen, J. E. ed. Federal world government. 280p. (Reference Shelf. v20, no5) H. W. Wilson Co. New York. '48.

League for Industrial Democracy. World cooperation and social progress: a symposium. 38p. The League. 112 E. 19th St. New York 3. '51.

Leonard, L. L. International organization. 630p. McGraw-Hill Book Co. New York. '51.

Levi, Werner. Fundamentals of world organization. 233p. University of Minnesota Press. Minneapolis. '50.

Lilienthal, A. M. Which way to world government? (Headline Series no83) 62p. Foreign Policy Association. 22 E. 38th St. New York 16. '50.

Lissitzyn, O. J. International court of justice; its role in the maintenance of international peace and security. (United Nations Studies no6) 118p. Carnegie Endowment for International Peace. 405 W. 117th St. New York 27. '51.

Morgenthau, H. J. In defense of the national interest. 283p. Alfred A. Knopf. New York. '51.

Pan American Union. Organization of American States and the United Nations. 22p. Supt. of Docs. Washington, D.C. '49.

Panikkar, K. M. and others. Regionalism and security. 73p. Indian Council of World Affairs. 8-A Kashi House, Connaught Pl. New Delhi, India. '48.

Parmelee, Maurice. Geo-economic regionalism and world federation. 137p. Exposition Press. New York. '49.

Perkins, Dexter. The story of American foreign policy. (Headline Series no90) 62p. Foreign Policy Association. 22 E. 38th St. New York 16. '51.

Perry, R. B. The citizen decides: a guide to responsible thinking in time of crisis. 225p. Indiana University Press. Bloomington. '51.

Taft, R. A. A foreign policy for Americans. 127p. Doubleday & Co. Garden City, N.Y. '51.

Ulman, Ruth, ed. University debaters' annual, 1950-51. 256p. H. W. Wilson Co. New York. '51.
    Non-Communist world organization. p9-44.

United States. Department of State. Toward a stronger United Nations. (International Organization and Conference Series 3) 64p. Supt. of Docs. Washington, D.C. '48.

United States. Department of State. Our foreign policy. (Publication 3972) (General Foreign Policy Series 26) 100p. Supt. of Docs. Washington, D.C. '50.

*United States. House of Representatives. Committee on Foreign Affairs. To seek development of United Nations into world federation; hearings on House Concurrent Resolution 64, October 12-13, 1949. 292p. 81st Congress, 1st session. Supt. of Docs. Washington, D.C. '49.
    Statement submitted by Grenville Clark, October 17, 1949. mimeo.

United States. Library of Congress. Legislative Reference Service. Atlantic pact. (Public Affairs Bulletin no69) 89p. Ap. '49.

United States. Senate. Committee on Foreign Relations. North Atlantic Treaty; hearings, April 27-May 18, 1949. 81st Congress, 1st session. Supt. of Docs. Washington, D.C. '49.

*United States. Senate. Committee on Foreign Relations. Revision of the United Nations Charter. 64p. (S. Report no2501) 81st Congress, 2d session. Supt. of Docs. Washington, D.C. '50.

*United States. Senate. Committee on Foreign Relations. Revision of the UN Charter; hearings, February 2-20, 1950. 808p. 81st Congress, 2d session. Supt. of Docs. Washington, D.C. '50.

*United States. Senate. The union of Europe. 44p. (S. Doc. no90) 82d Congress, 2d session. Supt. of Docs. Washington, D.C. '52.

Warburg, J. P. Last call for common sense. 311p. Harcourt, Brace & Co. New York. '49.

Ward, Barbara. Policy for the West. 312p. W. W. Norton & Co. New York. '51.

Wynner, Edith, and Lloyd, Georgia. Searchlight on peace plans; choose your road to world government. 532p. Dutton & Co. New York. '49.

PERIODICALS

Academy of Political Science. Proceedings. 24:181-90. Ja. '51. The international organization of the free world. Raymond Dennett.

Academy of Political Science. Proceedings. 24:367-76. Ja. '51. The organization of defense against aggression in the free world. Gladwyn Jebb.

*American Association of University Women. Journal. 43:135-43. Spring '50. World organization—the next step. B. A. Cohen and others. From UN to world federation. p 136-8. Cord Meyer, Jr.

American Journal of International Law. 45:538-9. Jl. '51. Need for a return to international law. P. B. Potter.

American Sociological Review. 16:749-57. D. '51. Sociology and the world crisis. R. C. Angell.

Annals of the American Academy of Political and Social Science. 280: 27-36. Mr. '52. International ideals and the national interest. F. L. Schuman.

*Business Week. p 101-5. Ja. 5, '52. Foreign policy: U.S. takes a new road.

Business Week. p21-2. Ja. 19, '52. World prosperity by fiat; economic report to Congress.

Catholic World. 174:326-31. F. '52. Taft, Acheson and the United Nations. Peter Berger.

*Christian Century. 69:179. F. 13, '52. United States domination in the UN weakening.

Christian Century. 69:270-2. Mr. 5, '52. Europe: time to reconsider.

Christian Science Monitor. p 17. Ap. 2, '52. Mouse, the lion, and NATO. A. E. Norman.

*Collier's. 129:22+. Je. 21, '52. United States of Europe. Beardsley Ruml.

Commentary. 10:507-17. D. '50. No German rearming without Atlantic union. R. H. S. Crossman.

Commentary. 12:226-31. S. '51. Beyond containment to liberation. Bogdan Raditsa.

Common Cause. 4:299-312. Ja. '51. Charter for Europe. R. W. G. Mackay.

Common Cause. 4:451-9. Ap. '51. Western regions and world federation.

Congressional Digest. 31:42-5. F. '52. Present day cause for concern.
    Entire issue devoted to growing conflict between the United States and the UN.

Congressional Record. 98:2351-5. Mr. 14, '52. Schuman plan and the integration of Europe.

Congressional Record. 98:A1778-9. Mr. 18, '52. Acres of diamonds. J. T. Wood.

Congressional Record. 98:1890-99. Mr. 24, '52. World government is a substitute for the UN. L. H. Smith.

*Congressional Record. 98:4570. Ap. 28, '52. Record of foreign aid. William Langer.

Contemporary Review. 180:218-23. O. '51. Implementing Atlantic union. G. E. G. Catlin.

Current History. 9:328-33. D. '50. European union or Atlantic union. R. C. Lawson.

*Current History. 21:331-6. D. '51. How necessary are cartels? V. E. Mares.

Current History. 22:13+. Ja. '52.
    Entire issue devoted to the UN, with special emphasis on United States policies.

*Current History. 22:39-46. Ja. '52. A report on the UN, 6th annual report to the General Assembly. Trygve Lie.

Current History. 22:161-5. Mr. '52. United Nations: new American relationship. R. W. Van Alstyne.

Current History. 22:216-20. Ap. '52. United Nations: disarmament and propaganda. R. C. Lawson.

Editorial Research Reports. 1:9-20. Ja. 2, '52. European unification. B. W. Patch.

*Editorial Research Reports. 1:241-56. Mr. 28, '52. Treaties and domestic law. B. W. Patch.

Foreign Affairs. 28:441-50. Ap. '50. European union: false hopes and realities. H. M. Lange.

*Foreign Affairs. 29:436-44. Ap. '51. Functional approach to European integration. D. U. Stikker.

Foreign Affairs. 30:1-16. O. '51. United to enforce peace. P. H. Douglas.

*Foreign Affairs. 30:175-87. Ja. '52. Security in the Pacific. J. F. Dulles.

Foreign Affairs. 30:188-96. Ja. '52. Pacific settlement seen from Australia. R. G. Menzies.

Foreign Affairs. 30:265-76. Ja. '52. Defense of Europe. H. J. Kruls.

Foreign Policy Bulletin. 31:4. O. 1, '51. Atlantic community economics. W. W. Wade.

Foreign Policy Bulletin. 31:3. Ja. 15, '52. How much authority for MSA? Blair Bolles.

Foreign Policy Bulletin. 31:3. Mr. 1, '52. Problems of a grand coalition. Blair Bolles.

Foreign Policy Reports. 26:66-80. Je. 15, '50. Western European union and the Atlantic community. J. P. C. Carey.

*Foreign Policy Reports. 27:50-61. My. 15, '51. Congress and the U.N. Carl Marcy and F. O. Wilcox.
    Includes Acheson plan for the UN.

Fortnightly 176:789-95. D. '51. Atlantic unity: time for decision. Kenneth Lindsay.

Fortnightly. 177:1-8. Ja. '52. ABC of Strasbourg. William Rydal.

Fortune. 43:121-4+. F. '51. U.S. foreign policy.

Fortune. 44:53-4. Ja. '52. The cost of being an American.

Freedom and Union. p8-1. N. '51. Logistics of Atlantic union. J. A. Mathews.

Freedom and Union. p18-20. N. '51. Possible step to Atlantic unity. Livingston Hartley.

Freeman. 2:397-400. Mr. 24, '52. Assault on American sovereignty. J. H. Ballew.

Harper's Magazine. 198:21-7. Mr. '49. World government—"Yes, but . . ." Chester Bowles.

International Affairs. 24:350-60. Jl. '48. Functional approach to world organization. David Mitrany.

International Affairs. 27:25-31. Ja. '51. The Council of Europe 1950. Maurice Edelman.

International Conciliation. 469:123-64. Mr. '51. Development of American regionalism: the organization of American states. A. P. Whitaker.

International Conciliation. 476:549-81. D. '51. International trade and economic nationalism. J. B. Condliffe.

International Organization. 4:236-46. My. '50. French view on security through international organization. Charles Chaumont.

International Organization. 4:383-99. Ag. '50. Congress and proposals for world government. P. E. Corbett.

International Organization. 4:573-84. N. '50. US, the UN and bi-polar politics. E. H. Buehrig.

International Organization. 5:274-81. My. '51. Impact of the UN on US foreign policy. B. V. Cohen.

Journal of Farm Economics. 33:601-12. N. '51. European economic integration and world trade policy. F. A. Knox.

Life. 32:36. Mr. 17, '52. Another subsidy? alas, it's needed.

Life. 32:24. Mr. 24, '52. Coexistence with Russia.

Nation. 174:265-7. Mr. 22, '52. United Nations or NATO? J. A. del Vayo.

New Republic. 126:9. F. 25, '52. Hurdles for atlanticism. Percy Winner.

Newsweek. 39:92. Mr. 24, '52. Are these handouts necessary? Henry Hazlitt.

*New York Times. p E6. N. 4, '51. Harriman has triple task in Europe. Felix Belair, Jr.

New York Times. p E6. D. 2, '51. Schuman plan as aid to European federation.

*New York Times. p E9. F. 10, '52. UN propaganda battle is regarded as a draw. T. J. Hamilton.

*New York Times. p E8. F. 24, '52. Death and birth at Lisbon.

*New York Times. p E5. Mr. 2, '52. Growth of NATO: from a Senate resolution to the Lisbon conference. James Reston.

*New York Times. p 14-15. Ap. 2, '52. Text of Eisenhower's first annual report to NATO as commander of West's forces.

*New York Times. p E5. Ap. 20, '52. U.S. joins reluctantly with colonial powers. T. J. Hamilton.

*New York Times. p E4. Ap. 27, '52. Europeans see a paradox in U.S. trade restrictions. M. L. Hoffman.

*New York Times. p E5. Ap. 27, '52. NATO assuming the place UN was expected to fill. T. J. Hamilton.

*New York Times. p E3. My. 11, '52. Europe asks questions on U.S. foreign policy. C. L. Sulzberger.

*New York Times. p28. My. 28, '52. Toward a new Europe.

*New York Times. pE5. Je. 1, '52. Now the U.S. frontier is fixed at the Elbe. James Reston.

*New York Times. p E5. Je. 8, '52. UN is facing mounting criticism in the U.S. T. J. Hamilton.

*New York Times. p E2. Je. 22, '52. Schuman treaty.

*New York Times. p E3. Je. 22, '52. Now the Schuman plan is nearer to reality. Harold Callender.

*New York Times. p E5. Je. 22, '52. A world balance sheet: two years after the attack in Korea. H. W. Baldwin.

New York Times Magazine. p7+. Jl. 22, '51. Containment is far from enough. Barbara Ward.
    Same abridged Independent Woman. 30:349+. D. '51.

New York Times Magazine. p 12+. Ag. 19, '51. Liberation, not containment. E. A. Gross.

New York Times Magazine. p 10-11. S. 9, '51. For Pax atlantica.

New York Times Magazine. p 13+. S. 23, '51. Europe moves slowly toward unity. Harold Callender.

New York Times Magazine. p7+. F. 3, '52. World investment, not foreign aid. P. G. Hoffman.

New York Times Magazine. p 12+. Mr. 16, '52. Wise men in search for security. T. H. White.

New York Times Magazine. p 10+. Ap. 27, '52. Answer to the critics of the U.N. E. A. Gross.

*Political Science Quarterly. 65:415-30. S. '50. The U.S., the Inter-American system and the U.N. E. S. Furniss, Jr.

Public Affairs. p 13-15. Autumn '51. Consolidating the free world. Ernest Davies.

*Reader's Digest. 60:71-2. Je. '52. Reexamining the UN. Walter Lippmann.

Reporter (Fortnightly). 4:17-20. N. 21, '50. World government. W. H. Hessler.

Reporter (Fortnightly). 5:9-11. F. 6, '51. To avoid encirclement, keep the balance of power. W. W. Kaufmann.

Reporter (Fortnightly). 5:4-5. O. 16, '51. The hope of Europe. Max Ascoli.

Reporter (Fortnightly). 5:4-5. D. 25, '51. Interlocking commonwealth. Max Ascoli.

Reporter (Fortnightly). 5:9-12. D. 25, '51. Motives for European unity. Louis Duval.

Saturday Evening Post. 224:20-1+. Ja. 5, '52. Can we remake the world without going broke? Demaree Bess.

Senior Scholastic. 60:16. F. 6, '52. Unite Europe now.

Senior Scholastic. 60:30. F. 20, '52. Other paths.

Senior Scholastic. 60:25. F. 20, '52. Regional organization.

Social Education. 16:61-4. F. '52. Atlantic union or else. W. E. Stevenson.

Social Studies. 42:147-52. Ap. '51. The council of Europe: an approach to European unity. M. B. Chatham.

United Nations Bulletin. 11:428-30. D. 1, '51. Prosperity through security. R. G. Casey.

United Nations Bulletin. 12:262-4. Mr. 15, '52. Proved instrument of European economic cooperation. Gunnar Myrdal.
   Economic Commission for Europe.

United Nations Reporter. 24:9-17. Mr. 25, '52. Five articles on various aspects of US-UN relations. B. V. Cohen, J. E. Shotwell and others.

United Nations World. 5:4-8+. N. '51. Alliance for peace or for war?

United States Department of State Bulletin. 24:523-8. Ap. 2, '51. Analysis of the Schuman plan.

United States Department of State Bulletin. 25:328-35. Ag. 27, '51. New approach to international security: economic cooperation. Nelson Rockefeller.

United States Department of State Bulletin. 25:771-4. N. 12, '51. UN and collective security. J. J. Sisco.

United States Department of State Bulletin. 26:91. Ja. 21, '52. Free world unity. J. F. Dulles.

*United States Department of State Bulletin. 26:155-9. F. 4, '52. What is Point Four? D. G. Acheson.

United States Department of State Bulletin. 26:275. F. 18, '52. Senate resolution endorses European federation.

*United States Department of State Bulletin. 26:710-12, 868-70. My. 5, Je. 2, '52. International organizations and conferences; calendar of meetings (cont).

*United States Department of State Bulletin. 26:960-7. Je. 16, '52. United States treaty developments.

United States Naval Institute Proceedings. 77:504-11. My. '51. Sovereignty is no giveaway gimmick. Harley Cope.

United States News & World Report. 31:56. Ag. 31, '51. Global job, a plan. David Lawrence.

United States News & World Report. 32:28-33. F. 1, '52. Europe's need: more self-help. R. B. Russell.

United States News & World Report. 32:22-4. F. 1, '52. General Eisenhower's latest size-up of the world situation. D. D. Eisenhower.

United States News & World Report. 32:84. F. 22, '52. Collective insecurity. David Lawrence.

United States News & World Report. 32:16. Mr. 21, '52. Lend-lease looked big; mutual aid is even bigger.

University of Chicago Round Table. p 1-16. Ja. 14, '51. The state of American foreign policy; radio discussion. W. T. R. Fox and others.

University of Chicago Round Table. p 1-16. Ag. 5, '51. How far should American and British foreign policy be coordinated? R. A. Butler and others.

University of Chicago Round Table. p 1-16. D. 2, '51. Should the UN be revised? Walter Johnson and others.

University of Chicago Round Table. p 1-18. F. 3, '52. How effective is the North Atlantic alliance? Walter Elliot and others.

*Virginia Quarterly Review. 27:179-95. Spring '51. What of the Council of Europe? W. G. Carleton.

Virginia Quarterly Review. 27:481-97. Autumn '51. Transatlantic misunderstanding. H. S. Hughes.

*Vital Speeches of the Day. 15:465-8. My. 15, '49. Reputation and performance in world affairs. J. F. Dulles.

Vital Speeches of the Day. 17:677-80. S. 1, '51. How can Europe unite? Sir A. E. Zimmern.

Vital Speeches of the Day. 17:680-3. S. 1, '51. Implementing the Atlantic pact. T. D. Cabot.

Vital Speeches of the Day. 18:67-8. N. 15, '51. Common foreign policy for Europe. R. Schuman.

Vital Speeches of the Day. 18:68-71. N. 15, '51. Unbreakable association of U. S. and Commonwealth. Lord Halifax.

Vital Speeches of the Day. 17:108. D. 1, '51. The integration of Europe. Konrad Adenauer.

Vital Speeches of the Day. 17:110. D. 1, '51. The story of the UN. J. T. Wood.

Vital Speeches of the Day. 18:194-7. Ja. 15, '52. How are we doing? D. G. Acheson.

Vital Speeches of the Day. 18:197-9. Ja. 15, '52. Organization of European defense community. Robert Schuman.

*Vital Speeches of the Day. 18:258-61. F. 15, '52. The year since the great debate. Herbert Hoover.

Vital Speeches of the Day. 18:324-7. Mr. 15, '52. Uniting Europe by peaceful means. D. G. Acheson.

*Vital Speeches of the Day. 18:368-70. Ap. 1, '52. Duty, honor, country. J. L. Collins.

Western Political Quarterly. 4:387-96. S. '51. The insecurity of states. N. J. Padelford.
    Includes a discussion of inadequacy of collective means of safety.

World Affairs. 5:70-87. Ja. '51. Strasbourg revisited. Susan Strange.

World Affairs. 5:88-102. Ja. '51. Atlantic union. Georg Schwartzenberger.

World Affairs. 5:129-44. Ap. '51. In praise of inconsistency. Susan Strange.

World Affairs Interpreter. 22:12+. Spring '51.
    Issue includes three articles on Organization of American States and its role in international affairs. S. S. Goodspeed, D. Rowlands, P. E. Hadley.

World Affairs Interpreter. 22:252-70. O. '51. Change and international organization. C. J. Schneider.

World Affairs Interpreter. 22:374-85. Ja. '52. Peace, but not at any price. Emmett O'Donnell, Jr.

World Affairs Interpreter. 22:349-61. Ja. '52. The quest for peace. P. G. Hoffman.

*World Affairs Interpreter. 22:402-14. Ja. '52. The organization of American States peace and power politics. Alexander DeConde.

Yale Review. 41:13-24. [S.] '51. Is the United States imperialist? Herbert Feis.

Yale Review. 41:194-206. [D.] '51. Wanted: wiser power politics. W. G. Carleton.

Yale Review. 41:234-46. [D.] '51. Communism in Western Europe. Mario Einaudi.